FROM DEMONS TO DRA

# FROM DEMONS TO DRACULA

## The Creation of the Modern Vampire Myth

MATTHEW BERESFORD

REAKTION BOOKS

*For Holly*

In Memory of Sophie Lancaster
(1986–2007)

Published by
REAKTION BOOKS LTD
33 Great Sutton Street
London EC1V 0DX, UK
www.reaktionbooks.co.uk

First published 2008, reprinted 2009, 2011
Copyright © Matthew Beresford 2008

All rights reserved
No part of this publication may be reproduced, stored in a retrieval
system, or transmitted, in any form or by any means, electronic,
mechanical, photocopying, recording or otherwise, without the prior
permission of the publishers.

Printed and bound in Great Britain
by CPI Antony Rowe, Chippenham, Wiltshire

British Library Cataloguing in Publication Data
Beresford, Matthew
From demons to Dracula : the creation of the modern vampire myth
1. Vampires
2. Vampires in literature
3. Vampire films
I. Title
398.2'1

ISBN 978 1 86189 403 8

# Contents

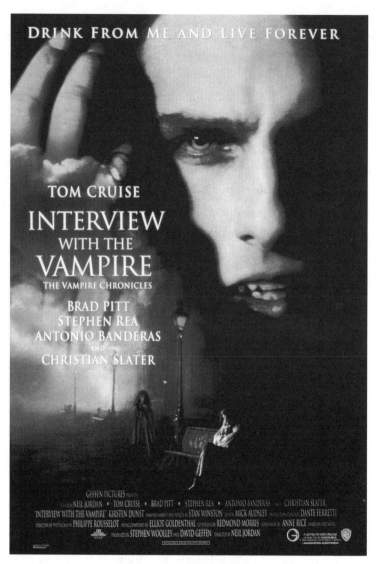

'Drink from me and live forever', advertising poster for the film adaptation of Anne Rice's *Interview with the Vampire*.

# Introduction

For, let me tell you, he is known everywhere that men have been. In old
Greece, in old Rome; he flourish in Germany all over, in France,
in India, even in the Chersonese; and in China, so far from us in
all ways, there even is he, and the peoples fear him at this day.
Abraham Van Helsing in *Dracula*

If ever there was in the world a warranted and proven history, it is
that of vampires: nothing is lacking, official reports, testimonials of
persons of standing, of surgeons, of clergyman, of judges; the judicial
evidence is all-embracing.
Jean-Jacques Rousseau

Belief in vampires is well documented throughout history, from
the shores of Ancient Greece and Rome to the wind-swept
deserts of Ancient Egypt; from Babylonia and India in the East
to France and England in the West. There are vampires in
Norse mythology, in the plagues and witch trials of the Middle
Ages, in the seventeenth-century 'Age of Reason' and in the
Gothic literature of Victorian England. So, too, the vampire
appears in modern times, in the emerging Dark Arts of the
Occult, the ever-growing Goth movement and in psychopathic
'vampiric' cases of torture, murder and blood-drinking across
Europe. As recently as 2002 a South African government official
was murdered by a gang claiming that the government was col-
luding with vampires.[1]

Evidence of vampires is certainly plentiful, and yet it
remains unclear what the evidence points to; what constitutes a
vampire? The *Collins Concise Dictionary* offers '1. (in European
Folklore) a corpse that rises nightly from its grave to drink the
blood of living people, 2. A person who preys mercilessly upon

others'; whereas the *Encyclopaedia Britannica* suggests that 'the persons who turn vampires are generally wizards, suicides, and those who come to a violent end or have been cursed by their parents or by the Church'. In the modern West the vampire takes the form of a somewhat aristocratic and seductive male, complete with cape and fangs, and with the ability to transform himself into a bat. This picture is, though, just a partial story; a reflection of the Victorian imagination, encapsulating all the charm and intrigue of high society with the added machinations of the underworld and an impression of the delightful debauchery that undoubtedly went on behind closed doors. To dissect this image is to uncover the real horror of the vampire, an evil that has tortured the human imagination for thousands of years. For, as Christopher Frayling suggests, the vampire 'is as old as the world'.[2]

The term 'vampire' first entered the English language in 1732, and came from the translation from German of the story of Arnold Paole, the first documented vampire case (discussed in detail in chapter Five). The etymology of the word suggests a transition through various languages. There are different suggestions of its origins, but the most likely contender is *upir* or *upyr* from the Slavic language, which in turn may have derived from earlier terms such as the Turkish *uber*, meaning 'witch'. This does seem quite feasible given the links between vampires and witches in East European countries. 'Vampire' is, however, merely the English variant of a much wider collection of terms denoting variants of the mythical being: in Romania the terms *moroi*, *strigoi* and *pricolici* are used; in Macedonia and parts of Greece *vrykolakas*; in Serbia *dhampir* and in Croatia *pijavica*. There are many more across the world. These terms and phrases often describe totally different beings. In the West, Romania is deemed by many to be the home of the vampire and yet Romanians themselves believe there are no vampires there at all; rather, as Dr Duncan Light agrees, they believe

Leaving for a witches' sabbat (after a painting by Teniers).

that Romania is the home of supernatural beings such as the aforementioned *strigoi*.

It is not just people who can become vampires either as, according to various superstitions, objects such as agricultural tools or other inanimate objects can turn into vampires if left outside on the eve of a full moon. The ethnologist Tatomir

Vukanović (1907–1997) even went so far as suggesting that certain types of fruit, namely watermelon and pumpkin, could become vampires. Vukanović 's accounts of the Serbian gypsies explain why this could be so:

> The belief in vampires of plant origin occurs among Gs. [gypsies] who belong to the Mosl. [Muslim] Faith in Kosovo-Metohija. According to them there are only two plants which are regarded as likely to turn into vampires: pumpkins of every kind and water-melons. And the change takes place when they are 'fighting one another'. In Podrima and Prizrenski Podgor they consider transformation occurs if vegetables have been kept for more than ten days: then the gathered pumpkins stir all by themselves and make a sound like 'brrrl, brrrl, brrrl!' and begin to shake themselves. It is also believed that sometimes a trace of blood can be seen on the pumpkin, and the Gs. then say it has become a vampire.[3]

Although the possibility of tools or vegetables turning into vampires seems beyond the limits of credulity, it is these deep-rooted superstitions that have given rise to the modern vampire myths. In reality, is this belief any less likely than people returning from the dead or transforming into bats? If Christians can believe that Jesus Christ was resurrected from the dead, then is the idea of vampiric resurrections really so preposterous?

There are many reasons why the vampire has remained in our conscious thought over time, but the one common element to almost all cases of vampirism is fear. Fear is an important factor in the survival of the vampire because, although the vampire has taken various forms in history, it is difficult to pinpoint one dominant form; fear is the main unifying feature, and therefore can be said to provide the key to the vampire's existence. One might say that *fear* of the vampire's existence is more important than its *actual* existence; 'Whether or not the demonic creature of our worst fears existed in fact, if we only looked into ourselves – and into our society – we should find the demon already there.'[4]

The fear within society, then, has led to a whole number of ways in which to prevent or defeat the vampire, from apotropaics such as garlic, holy water and rosary beads to power symbols such as the cross or, in some cases, crossroads. The practice of burying suspected vampires with crosses or at the junctions of crossroads is prevalent throughout Europe. Even as far back as the Roman period there is evidence of the dead being buried at crossroads; the reason for this, it is thought, is that if dead criminals or social outcasts were to come back to life, they would be confused by the abundance of paths, and thus be unable to find their way back to their village or town and cause further horror.

Recent work on the historical and cultural origins of the vampire suggests that:

> Our fears can make fantastic stories seem true. Humanity has often believed that we share our world with good or evil spirits, fabulous beings and strange creatures, sometimes helpful, sometimes menacing and vengeful. For centuries pain and illness were thought to be caused by evil spirits, which could be summoned by a witch or wizard (beliefs that still exist in some parts of the world). Fear of death, and of the souls of the departed being 'trapped' on earth, was at the origin of burial rituals. When these were not respected and something went wrong, the dead would not find peace and would come back to punish the living.[5]

It is these early ideas on death and ritual practices that allowed the creation of the vampire. Fundamental prehistoric rites such as excarnation (the de-fleshing of the body) and mummification opened the gateway to the spirit world that,

'A vampire rises from the grave...' in an eighteenth-century illustration.

once opened, would prove difficult to close. From ancient times to the present day, the world has been haunted by spirits, spectres, ghosts and monstrous beings. Whether these are real or imagined is irrelevant; it is the belief in them that enables their power over us. In many religions, to believe in good or God is to believe in evil or the Devil, and to deny this would be to upset the equilibrium of power. It has been suggested that the belief and superstitions of the Rroma Gypsies can be compared to other, heretical forms of Christianity, as 'the binary outlook on the world, including the opposition between pure and impure, is to be found, when relating to the supernatural, in a Manichaeist type of faith, not unlike the Persian dualism, in which both the powers of good, represented by God, and those of Evil, represented by the Devil, are complementary and equally necessary for the harmony of the world'.[6]

One has only to look at the monuments of the Neolithic period for evidence of belief in the spiritual world; it is suggested that cairns, for example, were placed on top of a grave to prevent the soul from escaping, thus allowing the spirit to roam free, and that grave goods were included with burials so the deceased could use them in the afterlife. In many cultures, such as those of Russia, Romania and other Balkan states, it is believed that the soul cannot be released from the flesh until the corpse has lain in the grave for some months; this is a point that is evident in the practice of excarnation in the prehistoric period.

Although the idea of vampires, or entities with vampiric qualities, can be traced back through time, it is not until the eighteenth century that any notable obsession with vampires can be witnessed, and it may be this fact that leads many vampire works to concentrate on this period onwards and, to some degree, to neglect what came before. Exactly what caused this phenomenon is difficult to fathom, but the course of the vampire was changed forever from the eighteenth century, and it is difficult to see significant changes in the vampiric being that emerged in the eighteenth and nineteenth centuries, or to imagine its changing into any other form in the future, a notion supported by the processes of modern technology, television and the internet. The vast numbers of books, plays, films and television programmes that incorporate the vampire in all manner of ways, from the nineteenth-century literature of *Dracula* and *Carmilla* to Anne Rice's *Interview with the Vampire*, from the early horror films starring Christopher Lee and Bela Lugosi to modern offerings such as *Blade* and *Buffy the Vampire Slayer*, and even to more lighthearted figures such as the Count in *Sesame Street* or the cartoon vampire duck *Count Duckula*, have all transpired to fix, possibly forever, the image of the vampire in modern times. The vampire is such a well-known figure at present that it is difficult to imagine a time when this was not the case.

A poster of *Buffy the Vampire Slayer*, the hit TV show that ran from 1997 to 2003.

Although the majority of people believe that the vampire is fictional or mythical, there are those that believe quite the opposite. The great debate on the vampire's existence reached its peak in the eighteenth century's 'Age of Reason', with discussion of it being an integral part of academic work. The Benedictine monk and scholar Antoine Augustin Calmet published his *Treatise on the Vampires of Hungary and the Surrounding Regions or The Phantom World* in 1746. On the then popular practice of tracking down and staking suspected vampires in their graves, we hear that

The cartoon vampire duck Count Duckula.

the stories told of these apparitions, and all distress caused by these supposed vampires, are totally without solid proof. I am not surprised that the Sorbonne has condemned the bloody and violent retribution wrought on these corpses; but it is astonishing that the magistrates and secular bodies have not employed their authority and legal force to put an end to it. This is a mysterious and difficult matter, and I leave bolder and more proficient minds to resolve it.[7]

Calmet may be contradicting himself by holding an opinion on the subject, as it was his belief that either there were vampires, in which case the evidence for them would be overwhelming, or there were not, and so the point of studying them was fruitless. Calmet's work was based on the hypothesis that there was an unparalleled relationship between the vampire and the evidence, that is to say, the accounts and evidence of eye-witnesses and the manifestations they purported to have seen.[8] But the acceptance of this 'evidence' could not possibly have been as clear-cut as this, particularly given the mass hysteria that was happening at the time on a scale not witnessed since the witch hunts of the Middle Ages. The Church's role in the legitimacy of the vampire at the time appears to be following some hidden agenda; Pierre-Daniel Huet, Bishop of Avranches (1630–1735), stated that 'I will not examine whether the facts of vampirism are true, or the fruit of popular error . . . but it is beyond doubt that they are testified by so many able and trustworthy witnesses.'[9] This appears to be an open admission by a leading figure in the Church that he believed the reports to be reputable and therefore accepts the existence of vampires, but then one must remember that there is a benefit to the Church in contrasting its goodness with the evil vampire. Is it coincidence that both the Revd Montague Summers, who wrote two important works on the vampire in the 1920s, and the priest Seán Manchester, the self-proclaimed exorcist of the 'Highgate Vampire', the only modern case of a vampire scare in England, are or were devout believers in the vampire?

The Church was not always willing to admit to the existence of vampires, however:

> Why is this demon so partial to base-born plebians? Why is it always peasants, carters, shoemakers and innkeepers? Why has the demon never been known to assume the form of a man of quality, a scholar, a philosopher, a theologian, a landowner or a bishop? I will tell you why. It is because men of education and men of quality are not so easily deceived as idiots of low birth and therefore do not so easily allow themselves to be fooled by appearances.[10]

Rousseau echoed these thoughts: 'For some time now the public news has been concerned with nothing but vampires . . .

yet show me a single man of sense in Europe who believes in vampires'.[11] And, despite all the supposed evidence and eye-witness accounts, no vampire has actually been caught in the act, so to speak, and no museum has acquired a specimen or any skeletal evidence.[12] However, believers would no doubt be quick to point out that an actual body or the remains of a vampire would be highly unlikely if the theory that aged vampires crumble to dust once killed is true, so this latter point of the argument can perhaps be explained away by vampire believers. It is quite feasible to suggest therefore that vampires are a creation of the imagination, and if one truly wants to believe one will make the evidence fit. The French philosopher Jean-Baptiste de Boyer's (1704–1771) explanations on the blood-like substance that was to be found in an alleged vampire are interesting, as he believed it related to nitrous particles in the soil being heated by the sun and mixing with fluids within the dead body.[13] Further suggestions for the explanation of vampire-like occurrences include plague victims, rabies, premature burials, slow-decaying corpses and a number of religious explanations such as heresies or area-specific superstitions. Such scientific attempts to debunk the vampire myth shall be considered in detail in chapter Five. There is in fact much evidence that seems to disprove the existence of vampires, and yet doubts still remain. As much as one dismisses the vampire, there is that curiosity buried deep in the mind, a desire to explore the mysteries of the inexplicable. It is that factor that has allowed the vampire to survive throughout the ages.

What follows, then, is a selective history of vampirism and its origins in an attempt to interpret the vampire's evolution and development into the modern vampire myth, from its early demonic form to today's caped and fanged harbinger of death.

Painting from a Greek vase showing Odysseus in the underworld, summoning the spirits of the dead by blood-sacrifice.

# ONE

# The Ancient World: Origins of the Vampire

I have dug up the sky, I have hacked up the horizon,
I have traversed the earth to its furthest extent,
I have taken possession of the spirits of the great ones, because I am
one who equips a myriad with my magic.
I eat with my mouth, I defecate with my hinder-parts,
for I am a god, lord of the Netherworld.
I have *given* those things which were established in the past,
I have planned appearance in glory.
Spell 10, *Egyptian Book of the Dead*

Torn from the Heavens, they fall from the sky and walk
the streets among mortal men
They hide in shadows, keepers of the night
Mortal life is weak, can't hold back the demons
The blood pours as rain and soon you'll be alone.
Misfits, 'Descending Angel'

Evidence of vampires, or beings with vampiric qualities, can be traced back as far as ancient Egypt, Greece and Rome and it is to these places that one must turn in order to understand the origins of the vampire. There is evidence which links vampiric beings in prehistory in all corners of the world, from ancient Babylonia to India, but Greece, Rome, Egypt and Eastern Europe are the most significant when tracing the vampire's roots. It is interesting to notice similarities in the vampire myth across differing countries and beliefs. In Croatia, Serbia, Romania and Macedonia there appears to be a moralistic element to the explanations for the creation of vampires: incest, non-baptism or birth outside of wedlock, for example. In Portugal and Russia there are links between vampirism and the occult, again suggesting a degree of religious intolerance. There are notable exceptions, however, that have no religious connotations: in Poland a person born with teeth was a child in danger of becoming a vampire, and in Eastern Europe people who were alcoholics in life were often dug up, staked, decapitated and had their hearts removed in the fear that they would become vampires in death. In Ireland there is evidence of the practice of placing stones on top of graves to prevent the deceased returning after death to the world of the living, a practice similar to the construction of cairns in the prehistoric period. The *lamiae* of Rome and Greece assumed the form of beautiful young women who would ensnare unwary young men and attempt to devour them; a serpent-woman is famously depicted in Keats's poem 'Lamia'. All these examples and beliefs, however, stem from the ancient traditions that laid the foundations for the modern vampire.

## THE LAMIAE OF ROME AND GREECE

In the story of the philosopher Apollonius of Tyana (*c.* AD 40–*c.* 120), we hear that 'this fine bride is one of the vampires, that is to say of those beings whom the many regard as lamias or hobgoblins . . . they are devoted to the delights of Aphrodite, but especially to the flesh of human beings'.[1] This describes the *empusas*, demons that assumed the body of a person.

Among tales of vampiric beings, children are a common theme. In various cultures, vampiric beings return from the dead to drink the blood of young children or devour them, such as the *obayifo* in Ghana, the *labartu* in Babylonia, the *aswang* in the Philippines and the *lamia, striges* and *mormos* in Rome, the servants of Hecate, goddess of witches. Indeed, the Roman writer Ovid mentions demons that would suck the blood of children and then devour them. It is suggested that the reason for the link with young children is due to the idea that their blood is still strong and pure,[2] an interesting theory, as the fixation

Herbert Draper,
*The Lamia*, 1909,
oil on canvas.

with blood as a life-source within many differing cultures is prevalent throughout history.

The vampires of Christianity, it would seem, also share this theme of blood, which can be seen as a distorted reflection of Mass, in which the blood of Christ has life-giving power.[3] Resurrection is also a common theme to both Christianity and vampirism. These similarities appear to suggest some definite links between the two. Furthermore, in Homer's *Odyssey,* Odysseus offers ram's blood to the spirits of the underworld, thus allowing them a short-lived renewal of life; and in Leviticus we hear: 'If any man whosoever of the house of Israel, and of the strangers that sojourn among them, eat blood I will set my face against his soul, and will cut him off from among his people: Because the life of the flesh is in the blood'.[4] One can theorize that the importance of blood, not just to the early examples of vampirism but to examples throughout its history, has evolved because 'the belief is, in all probability, linked up with the almost universal theory that transfused blood is necessary for revivification'.[5] The understanding of the importance of blood to the life force of any living creature from a very early point in history is perhaps the key to the universal link between vampirism and blood. Perhaps the most well-known blood cult is that relating to the Indian goddess Kali of *c.* 6th century BC onwards, who, as Kali Ma, is widely associated with the consumption of human blood. Members of the Thuggee cult carried out human sacrifices in the hope that by offering her blood freely, they would prevent her from taking it by forc.[6]

The Greek *vrykolakas,* a being with vampiric qualities, poses an interesting study, particularly as 'few cultures in the world have a vampire folklore tradition as long-standing, rich and carefully analyzed by scholars as Greece'.[7] The long pedigree of the Greek vampire myth, dating all the way back to classical times, gives us all the more reason to examine it. It is important to understand that there are two types of beings widely denoted as vampires; firstly, the supernatural, inhuman being such as demons or spectres; and secondly the revenant,[8] a human who returns to the world of the living after death. It is worth noting here that examples of 'vampires' from early periods generally take the form of the former, supernatural entity, and in later folklore traditions from the Middle Ages and beyond they adopt the form of the revenant, although there will undoubtedly be exceptions to this rule (for example, the Highgate Vampire of the 1970s took the form of the corporeal host, but was largely supernatural, with some attributes of the revenant). It is also evident that the vampiric revenant was only witnessed in Greece after the arrival of the Slavs in around AD 587,[9] and this appears to confirm the point that the earlier forms of vampire were not the traditional local kinds of undead being but a new import.

In addition to the examples of demonic creatures from ancient Greece, there are other areas that relate to the question of death and returning from death in some form. Customs in ancient Greece such as proper burial rites were so strongly believed in that even in battle opposing forces would honour each other's dead by allowing the bodies to be collected so the correct funerary rites could be performed (such as in the wars between Greece and Persia in the 5th century BC). Lawson, in his discussion of the idea of blood-guilt and vengeance pacts in ancient Greece,[10] states that in these cases, bodily return after death was expected to such a degree that murderers often mutilated the corpses of their victims by cutting off limbs in order to prevent them returning to seek vengeance. If they could return, they would then of course kill the murderer, who is thus also made a revenant who wreaks horrors on the living. This belief undoubtedly shares similarities with the typical vampire myth; the idea of a vampire attacking a person and transforming them into a vampire, who would then carry on this pattern, an idea that may come from the *vrykolakas*.

There are further suggestions that there are close links and evolutionary patterns among the ancient fables and myths (Homer's *Iliad* and *Odyssey*), classical writers (Plato, Sophocles, Virgil and Pliny the Elder) and later folklorists (from the medieval period onwards), and that the *vrykolakas* is a direct result of this evolution.[11] Indeed, while there are differences and similarities between cultural vampires, the *vrykolakas* is perhaps in some ways the atypical vampire creature in that it has held most or all of the 'vampire traits' at one time or another in its history, and is possibly the only vampire to have an obvious evolution or 'growth pattern' from its early demon form to the later revenant. In other countries, Romania for example, or in literature, we tend to see elements borrowed directly from the folklore of others, or attributes whose origins it is difficult to source.

From this we can conclude that for the ancient Greeks, the idea of returning in a state of 'undeath' caused real distress and a possible solution to this was a forced dissolution of cremation.[12] In some respects, and it must be pointed out that this is not a definitive theology, throughout the prehistoric and the historical periods (however these want to be interpreted), divisions into pagan and Christian, barbarian and civilized or dark and enlightened periods are reflected in funerary practices, most notably the replacement of cremation with inhumation. Therefore, one might see the dissolution of cremation and its replacement with inhumation ('to be left unburied was to be flung upon the cold earth, to be cursed as "incorruptible"'[13]) as the solution to vampirism. This would appear in the first instant to be a contradiction in terms, since if a body is cremated then there is nothing to come back after death (as one of the undead). However, according to Agnes Murgoci: 'In Russia, Roumania, and the Balkan states there is an idea – sometimes vague, sometimes fairly definite – that the soul does not finally leave the body and enter into Paradise until forty days after death'.[14] The thinking becomes somewhat clearer if one takes into account the belief that when a body is cremated the soul is instantly released and so may be malevolent. If a body is buried, however, natural decomposition is allowed, enabling the spirit of the deceased to travel into the next life once it is ready. This could explain Arthen's suggestion that cremation was aiding the vampire's existence. The shift in thinking on this issue is apparent, as nearly all modern depictions of vampires have them rising from the grave, a practice that would be impossible if cremation had not been replaced by burial.

The name *vrykolakas* has etymological links with the word 'werewolf', (English and German), 'warwulf' (Scottish) and 'loup-garou' (French). In Serbia it was thought that a person who was a werewolf in life would become a vampire in death. Indeed, the werewolf, or lycanthrope, is widely associated with the vampire in both folklore and fiction. Some believe that the term *vrykolakas* was borrowed from Slavic, meaning 'wolf' or 'pelt', and was originally used in Greece to mean werewolf,[15] as is still the case in some isolated remote villages in rural Greece. The suggestion here, then, is that the Greeks already had a tradition of vampire-like beings and applied an already existing term to the evolved vampire. It begs the question, however, why a term meaning wolf or werewolf would be attributed to an entirely different being, and this is still largely unanswered. There can be two possible reasons for this; firstly, that the documentary evidence for the links between the two have been lost or misinterpreted, or do not exist at all; and secondly, that rather than being a continuation of the early vampire tradition, the *vrykolakas* is an entirely new being that replaced the older supernatural vampiric beings. Both arguments are difficult to prove and much further examination of this is needed before any actual theories can be put forward. One thing that is certain is that although the vampire's later evolutionary history becomes somewhat problematic, its relevance within society does not. Vampire hunting was once so important a career in Greece that professional hunters were on a par with healers or scribes, and this reflects the extent to which the vampire had infiltrated society: 'People born on a Saturday (hence called "Greek Sabbatianoî" or Sabbatarians) are believed to enjoy the doubtful privilege of seeing ghosts and phantasms, and of possessing great influence over vampires . . . one was known to have lured a *vrykolakas* into a barn and to have set him to count the grains of a heap of millet . . . While the demon was thus engaged, the Sabbatarian attacked him and succeeded in nailing him to the wall'.[16]

In Roman mythology, Charon, the boatman of the River Styx, who carries the dead to the afterlife, takes his fee from the coin placed at burial either over the dead person's eyes or in the mouth. There is a suggestion that this theory is not the original reason for placing a coin in the mouth of the deceased, and that this original reason has been lost in classical literature.[17] It was thought that the soul escaped the body through the mouth, and could also return in this way, and so the placing of an offering, be it a coin, charm or piece of pottery inscribed with a magical pentacle, was a remedy against this returning. On the Greek island of Mykonos, this same magical pentacle was often carved on doors of houses to protect against the vampire; the placing of a token in the mouth of the deceased could be seen as a prevention of vampirism.

From ancient Rome there are also examples of the idea of vampirism concerning notable people from the period, the first being the emperor Caligula. It was reported that after having led a violent life and then suffering a violent death, Caligula returned to haunt the living. This could be due to the fact that his body was not given the proper burial rites but instead was semi-cremated and buried in a shallow grave. Pliny the Elder had his own ideas on burial; in particular, he believed that a large number of people who were thought to be dead and therefore buried were actually still alive, and his deep concerns on this are reflected in his *Historia Naturalis*: 'Such is the condition of humanity, and so uncertain is men's judgement that they cannot determine even death itself',[18] and this notion of premature burial can be witnessed in various countries throughout history.

Caligula, whose ghost is said to have haunted the Lamian Gardens until his burial rites were properly completed.

Pliny also mentions in this work examples from ancient Egypt and how the Pharoahs were known to have bathed in human blood to prevent diseases such as leprosy. Indeed, the customs and spiritual beings of ancient Egypt share some attributes with the ideas of vampires and vampirism, if they cannot be considered to be directly linked. One can find elements of these attributes in some of the spells from the most influential text on funerary practices from the time, the *Book of the Dead*. Spells 2, 9 and 180 are 'for going out into the day and living after death', while spells 27–29 are 'for not permitting a man's heart to be taken from him'. Spell 34 is a recipe 'for not being bitten by a snake in the realm of the dead', while spell 43 is 'for preventing a man's decapitation'. Spells 76, 85, 163 and 164 are 'for being transformed into any shape one may wish to take', 'for being transformed into a living soul' and 'for preventing a man's corpse

27

from putrefying', respectively. All these notions are in some way prevalent to vampire traditions; the removal of the heart and the head when killing a vampire, the transformation of a soul or living body after death, the shape-shifting and the biting of the flesh, and although these may well be mere coincidences, they nevertheless reflect early ideas that are still clearly associated with the vampire after several thousand years.

These spells and the results they were designed to give must have been serious issues in ancient Egypt and give an insight into how ideas on the afterlife were perceived. It is in ancient Egypt, some 4,500 years ago, that the first ideas on resurrection are witnessed. Resurrection was such a prominent issue that a technique of preservation was developed to maintain the condition of the deceased for their journey to the afterlife. Mummification was designed to preserve the dead in a state of 'suspended life' so the body would not decay and could live again in the next life. It is curious that the word mummification is derived from the Persian word *mummia*, meaning bitumen, as this mineral was renowned for its healing properties and was mistakenly associated with the dark resin coating of mummies by medieval travellers. In actuality, surviving documentary evidence from the period – such as the collection of embalmers' papyrus rolls and fragments, dated to 50 BC, from Hawara, an archaeological site in the Fayoum District, a 692 square mile depression in Northern Egypt known in prehistoric times as a lush paradise – give little detail of the substances used in embalming, except for general items such as jars of oils, linen strips, natron (a water-soluble alkali salt) and tools. Perhaps this silence intentionally creates an air of magic or mysticism and withholds the embalmer's secrets.

Regarding the chemical elements of the decay or putrefaction of a dead body, there are again certain elements that hold links with vampirism. The body decays due to bacteria in the intestines, which usually aid digestion, beginning the decompo-

Anubis reviving a mummified corpse.

sition process after death. With mummification, the internal organs are removed to prevent this decomposition. One of the first signs of putrefaction is a bloating of the body, and this occurrence is evident in a great number of 'vampire' cases whereby a suspected vampire is exhumed, only to be found in a bloated state, as if gorged on fresh blood. The gas that builds up within a putrefying body enters the blood cells and causes the skin to change colour, from a greenish hue through to purple and finally black, again witnessed in vampire traditions, where the skin of vampires takes on a deathly shade of purplish white. The release of these gases when a body is punctured, by a wooden stake for example, can also be used to explain the horrific smells attributed to the destruction of a vampire.

Ideas on death, burial, funerary rites and the afterlife are prominent in the ancient cultures of Greece, Rome and Egypt, but the mysticism of these ideas are somewhat lost to us due to the lack of documentary evidence, whether writings, inscriptions or hieroglyphs. One may, however, turn to the Stone Age and early Bronze Age to discover more about the mystic elements of death.

# TWO

# The Vampire in Prehistory: Early Ideas on Death and Burial

*Where there is mystery, it is generally supposed that there must also be evil.*

Christopher Frayling, *Vampyres: Lord Byron to Count Dracula*

The ideas of death and the afterlife were of major concern during both the Neolithic and Bronze Ages in Europe (5000–700 BC). The practice of excarnation (the defleshing of the body, usually by birds, to allow the release of the soul) was but one remedy thought to free the spirit, thus preventing the body from returning after death. Cremation was also prevalent in this period, where ideas on death and burial rites were intricate and complex and had to be strictly followed. It may also be the case that the prehistoric period holds the first actual evidence of a vampire, as a picture of a prehistoric bowl included in the journal *Delegation en Perse*[1] reflects a man copulating with a vampire whose head has been severed from its body.

According to Paul Barber in his book, *Vampires, Burial and Death*, there are four ways in which one could become a vampire. The first, predisposition, is caused when a person leads a violent life and has a violent death, such as with Caligula. The second, predestination, is caused when someone has no control over their destiny, for example, in the case of a child born out of wedlock or through incest, as in the Eastern European folklore traditions discussed earlier. The third is created by some form of violent event, such as the idea of murder in ancient Greece requiring mutilation of the corpse. And the final way to create a vampire involves incorrect practice of rituals and burial rites. This last method is the one most prevalent in prehistoric cultures.

Mentioned earlier was the act of placing stones on top of a grave to help 'contain' the dead, and evidence of these cairns are apparent in the Neolithic and Bronze Ages across Europe. They often differ in size and structure; the Clava cairns in the Highlands of Scotland, for example, are round mounds with centrally set stone chambers and an entranceway that opens to the southwest.[2] Examples in the Peak District of Derbyshire tend to be smaller and with a simpler structure, such as those at Beeley, Barbrook, Glutton and Eyam Moor. Cairns are remarkably similar in shape and composition to round barrows and often the two types merge. Technically speaking, a cairn is generally built entirely of stone (although this is often built up over an earthern mound) whereas a barrow tends to be purely an earthern mound but sometimes has an inner chamber of stone. The general progression across Europe is from large, chambered tombs or long barrows in the Neolithic period to much smaller cairns and types of smaller barrows in the Bronze Age. These structures represent a shift of funerary practices from, say, one large, communal burial mound used by a specific settlement or area in the Neolithic period, to more widespread, isolated, round barrows used to house the dead of a particular family, for instance, in the Bronze Age.

In the Neolithic period, although there are quite a number of chambered tombs and long barrows evident across Europe, there are not nearly enough to have housed the population, leading to the suggestion that these burial chambers may have been reserved for society's elite. This is not necessarily the case.[3] What we do notice, however, is that more often than not it is the leg bones or the skulls that are housed within the tomb as a symbolic gesture of burial, rather than a body being found there in its entirety. This is not to say that complete burials are not found within the tombs, but the majority of internments are partial or incomplete. This could also be true of the practice of cremation, as the extreme temperatures required for total cremation had not yet been mastered in the early prehistoric period and so bodies were only part-cremated; again, perhaps, a symbolic burial.

Not until the Bronze Age, when technology advances led to greater understanding of heating temperatures and control over fires and kilns increased, do we see new capabilities in 'complete' cremations. Generally, therefore, we witness a divide between inhumation in the Neolithic period and cremation in the Bronze Age. As regards inhumation, knowledge of bodily decomposition rates in various soil types, in particular clay or waterlogged soils where decomposition would be slow, were certainly known from at least the Neolithic period,[4] and so we might expect to find areas of poorer soil types void of burials. If not, bodily preservation could have occurred, or at least a delayed decomposition, and given the specific burial rites evident from the period this could have caused problems. In the eighteenth and nineteenth centuries we see that those buried within the areas of graveyards with poorer soil compositions are generally social outcasts such as suicides, adulterous women and murderers. These almost certainly resulted in delayed decay, which may have given the appearance of vampirism. Early understandings of soil types must have been crucial when burial practices were such an integral part of society.

In the early prehistoric era, there is a notable change in burial attitudes, particularly towards inhumation. Burial, along with the interment of grave goods, replaced cremation, and this inhumation then progresses from 'communal' chambered tombs, such as West Kennet Long Barrow in Wiltshire, into more nucleated burials in much smaller barrows as the transition from the Neolithic into the Bronze Age takes place. Once in the Bronze

Inside the Hazleton chambered tomb.

Age, cremation once again becomes the preferred method. The complex burial rites of the period are all too apparent.

In Britain there appears to be a clear north / south divide, with the majority of monumentation situated in the south, particularly in the area around Wiltshire, and this most likely reflects soil and landscape diversities. Particularly important as regards burial practices are the chambered tombs of West Kennet and Hazleton North, both belonging to the Cotswold–Severn tradition. Excavations at West Kennet in the 1950s of four of the five chambers of the tomb (the fifth chamber had been excavated a century earlier) revealed the disarticulated remains of at least 46 individuals and, perhaps surprisingly, at least two cremation burials.[5] Similarly, between 33 and 40 individuals were discovered at Hazleton, along with two cremations. The figures are remarkably similar at both sites, but the obvious parallels do not end there. At both sites the cremation burial deposits were located near to the entranceway and, given that we know that cremation was prevalent in the *later* prehistoric era, this could have been symbolic of a specific rite, or may relate to the closure of the tomb in the Bronze Age[6] (the main feature of a chambered tomb was that not only was it a communal burial site, but it was also left open for prolonged periods to allow further burials to be accommodated). Clearly there was a structured and widely understood process in the prehistoric period.

In *The Buried Soul,* Timothy Taylor discusses the beliefs attributed to early burial rites, and in particular the idea that early man at some point recognized the separation of the soul and body. After death, therefore, the soul may attempt to reassert itself with its worldly body and retrieve its 'possession', but only while the flesh remained on the body. After the flesh no longer remained, the soul would have no choice but to move on to the afterlife (as with later beliefs noted in Russia and Romania, for example). This would explain the attempts to suspend the body's natural state, such as in mummification, in an

Excarnation platform at Dra Yerpa monastery, Tibet, 1921.

attempt at immortality. At an early point humans must have recognized the question of the immortal soul, and come to the belief that our time on earth within the body was merely a stage in an everlasting existence. Those who buried human remains with these rites and rituals must have had the belief that something happened after death, and this is supported in the exposure platforms and in excarnation, which allow the soul to escape once the flesh has gone.[7] We can assume that if these peoples believed that their soul travels on to the next life, then they must also have believed that there must be some form of higher order, or at least that an unknown power enabled these progressions between lives. On the surface it appears that the link between religion and burial rites is present, particularly in earlier times, as reflected by the great monuments of the prehistoric period, such as Stonehenge or Wiltshire's Silbury Hill. Perhaps these monuments were the prehistoric equivalent of modern churches or mosques.

In the Iron Age, ideas on death and burial remained similar, but it was the practice that altered, notably in the bog bodies from the period. Examples from Ehrenberg in Bavaria show, like previous examples, fear of the dead returning. Here, a woman was buried with a large stone on top of her and a man was also buried face down, weighted with a heavy rock. It is almost as if these were precautionary measures taken to prevent the dead's return. There is also a curious example from the Iron Age in the bog body of the Lindow Man discovered just south of Manchester in 1984. Apart from a fox fur armband, Lindow Man was naked. This armband provoked interesting debate; although its actual purpose is unclear, there are varying suggestions of what

The Lindow Man bog body.

it may represent, such as the theory that Lindow Man's name could be Fox, based on the name Lovernios (meaning 'fox'),[8] or Leslie Ellen Jones's suggestion that it signifies that he was a human sacrifice.[9] The wearing of a fox fur armband in medieval Europe was symbolic of the wearer being a lycanthrope or vampire and was linked with the ability of shapeshifting.[10] This could explain the brutal death and burial of Lindow Man, but, more importantly, if true, reflects an extremely early example of the fox fur / vampire relationship. Many of the bog bodies also shared parallels with vampirism, in that a great many were pinned down into the bogs by having stakes driven through them.

With the transition from the Neolithic and Bronze Ages into the Iron Age and later, there appeared to be a shift in attitudes regarding not only death and burial customs but also the monuments attributed to these. In his *Folklore of Prehistoric Sites in Britain* Leslie Grinsell explains this shift: 'it is generally accepted that the god of one religion becomes the Devil of that which replaces it. From this it follows that from the introduction of Christianity onwards, the monuments of earlier times began to be attributed to the Devil'.[11] From this early period almost all monuments came to be viewed in this way, from the chambered tombs and barrows to the standing stones, linear ditches and stone circles, and these monuments often share links with occult practices in the present. The word 'Grim' is often associated with the Devil, and according to Grinsell, many of the linear ditches from the Prehistoric bear the interchangeable names Grim's Ditch or Devil's Ditch. Examples of these 'Grim's Ditches' are evident in widespread places such as Dorset, Hampshire, Norfolk, Oxfordshire, Wiltshire and Hertfordshire. Grim also has links in other contexts, however, notably from the later Saxon and Viking periods, where Grim was used as another name for Woden, and 'grima' applied to a spectre or goblin. There are much earlier examples of the use of the word Grim at Grimes Graves, the Neolithic flint mines, and the mound of Grim's Hoe, both in Norfolk. It is likely that this word could have been applied to these places in later times to link them with the Devil in accordance with Grinsell's argument. It is also interesting to note that all the examples of Grim's Ditches mentioned lie south of what later became the Danelaw boundary, that is, within the Saxon lands. Grinsell also mentions that 'Saxon land charters embodying the word "scucca" (goblin or demon, especially Satan) may relate to the Devil, e.g. Shucklow (the Devil's Barrow) in Buckinghamshire'.[12]

There is clearly some relationship with the Devil, even if in a derogatory sense, creeping into society at this point in history, and as shall be seen from this period onwards, this bears direct relevance to the vampire's evolution, particularly in the Middle Ages. All the early examples are perhaps better described as vampiric beings rather than vampires in the true meaning of the word; that is, they have some of the qualities of a vampire, but cannot necessarily be identified with the modern vampire. The question here is whether the vampire actually *existed* in the human imagination up until this point. In order to attempt to answer this question, one must examine the set of beliefs and practices that grew alongside the modern 'vampire' from this period onwards: Christianity.

The Devil Tarot card.

# THREE

# Historical Roots: The Vampire in the Middle Ages

Vamp²: vb vamp up to make (a story, piece of music, etc) seem new
by inventing additional parts
*Collins Concise Dictionary*

I tell you, you walk this earth as all evil things do, by the will of God,
to make mortals suffer for his Divine Glory. And by the will of God
you can be destroyed.
Anne Rice, *The Vampire Lestat*


'One morning we came down to find in the middle of the par-quet floor of the sitting room the mark of a single cloven hoof in mud. The house and windows were very small, so it was quite impossible for an animal to get in . . . [or] leave one single footprint. We hunted everywhere for a second trace but without success'.[1] Montague Summers (1880–1948), leading vampirologist and Catholic priest, describes this incident as being a 'vampiric experience' and that the evil force involved was 'something old and waning that had not a sufficient reserve of new strength'. Being a devout believer in the vampire, it is perhaps understandable that he immediately associated this experience with vampires, yet the mention of the cloven hoof conjures images of a different 'evil' being in the minds of most: the Devil. From the period of Christ onwards, and as Christianity has evolved, this link between the vampire and the Devil becomes all too apparent. Whether the vampire is seen as a manifestation of the Devil or merely a creature in league with him is often unclear, and this could well be down to the vampire's pagan origins as considered from a Christian perspective. After all, as Montague Summers puts forward in his 1928 introduction to the *Malleus Maleficarum*, perhaps the best-known medieval treatise on witches and witch-hunting, 'at the time of the triumph of Christianity a decadent Empire in the last throes of paganism was corroded by every kind of superstition and occult art, from the use of petty and harmless sympathetic charms of healing to the darkest crimes of goetic [demonic] ceremonial'.

As we have seen, there are clear foundations for the vampire in the ancient world, and it is impossible to prove where the myth first arose. There are suggestions that the vampire was born out of sorcery in Ancient Egypt,[2] a demon summoned into this world from some other. From a Christian point of view, the vampire's creation can be directly linked to the story of Christ himself through Judas Iscariot. Certain elements of the story of Jesus's betrayal to the Romans by Judas have direct links to the modern vampire myth, leading to the suggestion that Judas can be considered the first vampire. The idea that Judas's betrayal was the ultimate act of antagonism towards Christianity could explain why the vampire is seen as such an evil creature by the Church throughout history, but there are more obvious elements: the crucifix or cross, revered and feared by the vampire; the stake, with its similarities to the nails forced through Jesus's hands and feet, pinning him to the cross; and the silver, which the vampire loathes, and which Judas accepted in payment for betraying Jesus. Judas returned the silver coins after his turn of conscience, which could explain why the vampire hates silver, a detail that is not common in folklore (where iron tends to be the significant metal for preventing evil, often in the form of amulets or nails worn around the neck).

Other vampiric associations with Judas include red hair, which is prominent in Greek vampires; the fact that Judas hanged himself, and that suicides are linked with vampires, as discussed in chapter One; and the 'kiss of Judas', which identified Jesus to the Romans, and which can be associated with the 'vampire's

*The Suicide of Judas*, by Gislebertus, *c.* AD 1120. Stone carving from the Cathedral of Saint-Lazare, Autun.

kiss', or the biting of the throat. The field in which Judas hanged himself is known as the *Akeldama*, or 'field of blood', in the Acts of the Apostles, and the links between Christianity and blood, and vampires and blood, are obvious. Judas is the first vampire in Wes Craven's film *Dracula 2000*, where Judas was portrayed as unable to truly die and forced to be undead forever as he was without the forgiveness of God. He is also considered the first vampire by a vampiric cult known as 'The Children of Iscariot' in Eastern Europe. The French author Paul Féval, in his 1875 novel *La Ville-Vampire* ('Vampire City'), calls one of the rulers of the vampires Baron Iscariot, clearly emphasizing his links with Judas. Whether there is any truth in the idea that the vampire, in the modern sense of the word, was created by the Church or by Christians as a symbol of evil based on the betrayal of Judas, is impossible to know. The similarities may be mere coincidence, but it is certainly curious that elements such as the cross, the stake, the suicide and the blood are almost always present in vampire traditions as well as other factors such as red hair, silver and knots (an element of hanging). It is only other apotropaics such as mirrors, garlic and seeds that are not contained in the Judas theory, but these are prominent in folklore or literature and are most likely later additions. This is not to say that the vampire was created very early in Christian history, as it could have appeared as late as the seventeeth and eighteenth centuries, when the interest in vampires was at its peak. The vampire is therefore a (heretical) scapegoat of Christianity, in much the same way as witches were in the Middle Ages, and perhaps did not become applied to secular ideology until the most well-known vampire, the caped and fanged vampire of literature, was created.

In Dante's *Inferno*, Dante and Virgil travel through the nine Circles of Hell, the Devil's lair. Each of the nine circles represents a sin; Circle One, Virtuous Pagans and the Unbaptized; Circle Two, The Wanton; Circle Three, The Gluttonous; Circle Four, The Avaricious; Circle Five, The Irascible; Circle Six, The Heresiarchs; Circle Seven, The Violent; Circle Eight, The Fraudulent and Malicious; and Circle Nine, Traitors to their Lords and Benefactors. Now consider the vampire; anti-Christian, cruel, destructive, insatiable, greedy, easily angered, heretical, violent, fraudulent and malicious. And then the ninth Circle: traitorous. Dante and Virgil escape the bowels of Hell by climbing down the legs of Lucifer, the triple-headed Satan, each mouth chewing a traitor for eternity. On the right and left sides are Cassius and Brutus, conspirators against Caesar, and in the middle 'that soul up there that has the greatest pain', Judas Iscariot.[3]

The Church plays an important role in vampirism and can often be seen to use it for its own purposes. Greek Christianity is wrongly accredited with starting the vampire phenomenon, although the belief was 'undoubtedly developed greatly' by the Greek Church and Greek priests used it as an 'additional power over the people'.[4] This is most certainly true in almost all Christian countries at some point; as has been stated above, the Church can make use of pitting itself against evils, and the vampire fits this requirement perfectly, but its roots undoubtedly lie deeper in the past.

In Crete a person believed to be a vampire had most often led an evil life or had been excommunicated by the Church, and after death the body would become possessed and would grow in power over 40 days. This is curious, as in Orthodox death lore, 40 is a prevalent number, and is the length of time between the death of Christ and his ascension to heaven. (It is also the amount of time Jesus spent being tempted by the Devil in the desert.) The idea of suicide within Christianity and the belief that to commit suicide was to defy the will of God is another example of a way that a person could become a vampire, and it is known that the burial of suicides was forbidden within consecrated ground. It is interesting that in the 2005 film *Kingdom of Heaven*, depicting the Crusades and the fight for the Holy Land, a woman who had committed suicide had her head cut off before burial; this practice itself has links with vampirism, as in folklore one way of destroying a vampire was to cut off its head. It is possible that the Church used society's fear of becoming a vampire in order to deter suicides.

It was perhaps in the period when Christianity replaced various pagan religions and practices as the primary religion in the Saxon period that the vampire as we know it began its emergence into wider society. The folklore and superstitions of the medieval periods as a whole, from the early medieval period of the Saxons to the later medieval Middle Ages, can be seen as

Statue of Jesus on the cross at Rasnov Fortress, Romania.

the foundations of this modern vampire. They were themselves derived from earlier fears and obsessions with demons, spirits and death. Indeed, a possible origin of the vampire is from a folkloric rendering of the Christian Cain and Abel story. Cain killed his brother Abel and so was banished; he wandered until he met Lilith, the original partner of Adam, who had left Adam and become a witch. Lilith had become a mother to demons in a bargain made with the angels. She is often depicted as killing human children and showed Cain the life power of blood. Cain is later referred to in the New Testament as being 'the prototype of the wicked man'. In some ways he bears similarities to Judas, in that he betrayed and ultimately killed his brother: the similarity can be drawn even though there is a difference in that, with Cain and Abel, this was a literal brotherhood, whereas in the Jesus and Judas version the brotherhood was figurative.

Of course, this is not an orthodox Christian belief. Cain is only mentioned briefly after Genesis, in the New Testament, and Lilith is not mentioned at all in the Bible. In the Anglo-Saxon epic poem *Beowulf*, when the reader learns of the poem's evil monster, Grendel, it is explained that Grendel 'had dwelt for a time in misery among the banished monsters, Cain's clan, whom the Creator had outlawed and condemned as outcasts . . . the Almighty made him [Cain] anathema and out of the curse of his exile there sprang ogres and elves and evil phantoms'.[5] As *Beowulf* was written somewhere between the middle of the seventh and end of the tenth century, some 600–900 years after the birth of Christ, the parallels with early Christian parables within a widely Pagan adventure are intriguing. Although the poem appears to be from a pagan perspective, there are arguably Christian elements; for example when Shield Sheafson dies he is laid in a boat with grave goods and cast out to sea, a pagan tradition, but it is mentioned that Shield 'crossed over into the Lord's keeping',[6] presumably the Christian Lord. In addition, it can be argued that Christian philosophy permeates the poem; unselfishness is prized, for example, and it is understood that all earthly blessings originate from the gods.

Later in *Beowulf* we hear that Grendel's mother; 'had been forced down into fearful waters, the cold depths, after Cain had killed his father's son, felled his own brother with a sword.

Branded an outlaw, marked by having murdered, he moved into the wilds . . . and from Cain there sprang misbegotten spirits, among them Grendel, the banished and accursed'.[7] This description is markedly similar to that above and one wonders why the poet felt the need to reiterate the point that Cain's wrongdoings led to the creation of evil beings. Indeed, the inclusion of Cain in *Beowulf* is curious and it is interesting to note the poet's apparent hatred towards Cain; in the Bible this animosity is not present even after Cain's banishment. Also, given the fact that *Beowulf* originated in the form of an oral poem and was much later transcribed and re-transcribed by the literate, that is, Christian monks, it is most interesting that these references to Cain as a progenitor of evil remained – or indeed this may be when they first appeared. One can only assume that there was a resonance with this in the period when *Beowulf* was composed that has been lost to us.

Throughout the early medieval period there are references to what can only be described as 'vampiric incidents' (one must remember here that the caped and fanged vampire did not yet exist and it is the 'folkloric' vampire that was the predominant guise). The Danish historian Saxo Grammaticus in Book I of his *Gesta Danorum* mentions that Odin was attacked and slain by the inhabitants of Finland when he travelled there. After his death he continued to cause 'abominations' and spread pestilence until the locals removed his body from his burial mound, beheaded it and drove a sharpened stake through his heart, after which they found relief.

In Book II, Grammaticus tells the story of Aswid and Asmund, two friends who die and are buried together, along with Aswid's horse and dog. Asmund promptly returns to life, rising from the grave and proclaiming that Aswid had devoured both horse and dog and turned his appetite onto him. In response, Asmund cut off his head and 'impaled his guilty carcase with a stake'.[8] Whilst discussing the early history of vampires, Old Catholic Bishop and self-styled vampire hunter Seán Manchester points out that during the Anglo-Saxon period in England a law was passed that allowed wooden stakes to be driven through any person suspected of being undead (it is important to note that the law specified 'undead' rather than 'vampiric',[9] suggesting that the beings feared in these early periods were not associated with what we would deem a vampire to be today), and that this law was only repealed in 1823.

It is apparent that as in the medieval period there was a growing interest in the phenomenon of the dead rising from their graves, in an era known throughout feudal Europe as the 'Age of the Antichrist'.[10] William of Malmesbury explains that this is due to the reanimation of evil men after their deaths by the Devil, who 'compels them to act as he desires'. In *Historia rerum anglicarum* ('History of English Affairs') William of Newburgh (1136?–1198?) recounts many instances of the dead returning from their graves to harass family, friends and neighbours.[11] It is interesting that the common factor to all the tales, folklore and superstitions from across Europe is that they are almost uniquely of a peasant origin, and one would therefore wonder how these traditions, which are markedly similar across the spectrum, travelled across a wide area in such a short space of time, given the relative immobility of the peasant classes of the period.

It has been claimed, for example by Seán Manchester, that both the Eastern and Western churches accepted the existence of vampires, which may go some way to explaining the spread of the idea of vampires. This is supported by the fifteenth-century book *Malleus Maleficarum* ('Witch Hammer'), described as being 'influential in establishing vampirism as one of the worst manifestations of the Devil'.[12] For, as Montague Summers suggests 'if the disease is universal, the medicine must be sharp'.[13] It is a kind of manual for witch-hunters, and thoroughly details almost every possible aspect of witchcraft, from the

Witch trial.

perversions undertaken by prospective witches, to methods used to track them down, and methodology for defeating the 'Devil's work', that is, witchcraft. Yet under the surface, one can also find examples of traits we associate with vampirism, particularly in relation to the Devil's ability to adopt the form of another person or control their mind, which in either case leads to the ability to misguide the victim into committing malevolent acts. The authors, Johann Springer and Henrich Kraemer, both Inquisitors and members of the Dominican Order, created in the *Malleus Maleficarum* such an influential work that it was used by all, from clergy to judges, to hunt out, torture and condemn thousands of innocent 'witches' during the Middle Ages.

The mass hysteria created by such a fervently naïve population allowed for one of the worst atrocities in history. In a narrative on the links between vampires and religion it is suggested that 'the Church in Europe during the Middle Ages came to recognize the existence of vampires and changed it from a pagan folk myth into a creature of the Devil. The vampire, though clearly a thing of evil and a pagan myth, had its believability reinforced by pre-existing Christian doctrines.'[14] The Church recognized in the vampire an opportunity that could be used as a tool in furthering its own strength. The only differ-

A 1570s engraving of a witch-burning.

ence between vampires and witches is that vampires could not be found and slain, yet the tragedy is that any woman or man could have been put to death as a witch, so long as there was 'evidence', be it a tortured confession or a 'heretical gift' such as the power of healing or herbology. It proved somewhat difficult to punish the undead harasser or blood-drinking fiend, and so the educated could dismiss the vampire myth which was so prevalent among the peasants, as they saw no evidence for it.

It would take the 'Age of Reason and Enlightenment' to finally expose the vampire to all parts of society, fuelled largely by the European vampire epidemics of the eighteenth century. These were able to take hold in the West largely because the

Torturing witches.

vampire was reincarnated as a being that was relevant to that area of society that had ridiculed the peasantry for their beliefs in the fiend for so long: the learned. Before we can understand this newfound interest we must look towards the heartland of the epidemics to a place deemed by many to be the home of the vampire, the area around Transylvania in modern-day Romania, where many of the Eastern folklore roots have their origins.

FOUR

# Vampiric Haunts #1:
# Transylvania, Romania

We are in Transylvania, and Transylvania is not England. Our ways are
not your ways, and there shall be to you many ſtrange things.
Count Dracula, *Dracula*

Transylvania might well be termed the land of superſtition,
for nowhere else does this curious crooked plant of delusion
flourish as persiſtently and in such bewildering variety.
It would almost seem as though the whole species of demons,
pixies, witches, and hobgoblins, driven from the rest of Europe
by the wand of science, had taken refuge within this mountain
rampart, well aware that here they would find secure lurking-places,
whence they might defy their persecutors yet awhile.
Emily de Lazowska Gerard, *The Land Beyond the Foreſt*

These descriptions of Transylvania conjure images of a strange
and mysterious place inhabited by mystical beings, a safe haven
for the Underworld's brood. The very name 'Transylvania' is
synonymous in the West with a dark and misty land peaked by
mountains and home to blood-sucking fiends. My own first
glimpse of Transylvania did not disappoint; the snow-capped
Carpathians were shrouded by an early morning mist and the air
felt a good few degrees colder upon entering 'vampire country'.
Indeed, everything felt somewhat darker and more foreboding
than the Wallachian gateway to the south. Areas such as Yadu
Drakuluj ('the Devil's Abyss') and Gregynia Drakuluj ('the Devil's
Garden'),[1] nestled amongst thickly-forested plateaus, do little
to alleviate this opinion.

It is suggested that somewhere atop these mountains is the
legendary *scholomance* or 'magic school' where the secrets of
nature, magic spells, incantations and charms are taught by the

The Carpathian Mountains, gateway to Dracula country.

Devil. Legend has it that only ten people are permitted at any one time, of whom only nine return; the tenth is taken by the Devil himself in payment for the mysteries offered. This hapless individual from then on spends their life riding a dragon through the skies and preparing thunderbolts for future storms.[2] Further traditions attribute magical capabilities to a whole number of animals such as the swallow (luck-bringer), sheep (highly prized and capable of predicting danger), crow (evil omen), cuckoo (an oracle, often depicted as a spirit of a lover within Romanian poetry), toad (often in the service of a witch), hare (brings bad luck when crossing your path) and fox or wolf (which brings good luck when crossing your path).[3] In light of these superstitions regarding animals, it becomes easier to understand the fears and superstitions attributed to spirits (and in turn beings such as vampires, witches and werewolves). Often these spirits have a supernatural quality, such as the *strigele*, which is said to be the spirit of a witch and can be seen as little specks of light floating in the air.[4] These specks of light are often reported in cases of supernatural activity but within Romanian folklore they usually lend themselves to the belief that they are a soul or spirit.[5] In parts of Transylvania a butterfly flitting about is thought to be a projection of a person's soul and in Valcea there is a similar belief that the souls of vampires are carried in death's-head moths. Tradition has it that these should be impaled with a tiny pin and fixed to a wall. The spirit or soul of a person plays a big part in Romanian funerary beliefs and traditions and from this follows the general belief that dead bodies should be disinterred as follows: in the case of a child, three years after death; in the case of the young, after four or five years; and in the case of the elderly, after seven years.[6] After these periods it is thought that the bones should be clean of flesh, signifying the soul's release into eternal rest, and the bones should then be washed in wine and water and re-interred. If the body has not fully decomposed in the set period, it is traditionally believed that the person is a vampire. Generally speaking, the vampire in Romanian folklore tends to be a mischievous pest that causes trouble and plays tricks upon people, although from time to time there are examples of them being malevolent and causing pain, injury or sometimes death. Wider studies on the folklore of the Carpathians, which encompass parts of Transylvania,[7] the Czech Republic, Poland, Austria, Ukraine, Slovakia and Russia, depict examples of vampires chasing and scaring horses, stealing wood and causing rough waters on rivers by beating the water with great boards,[8] rather than attacking people and drinking their blood, as they do in the West. Belief in these vampires, spirits, witches and demons is extremely prevalent and widespread, encompassing many of the countries in the Carpathian area of Eastern Europe. Bogatyrev confirms that 'the belief in apparitions and in supernatural beings, as well as in the power of sorcerers or of magical ceremonies, is still completely alive among the peasants of the

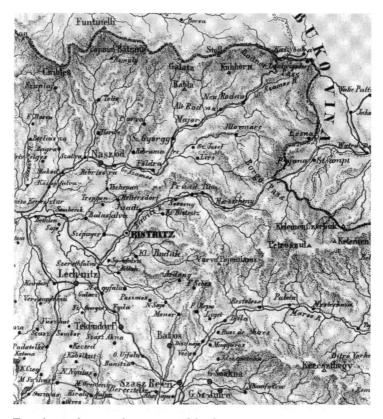

Transylvania, from a 19th-century guidebook map.

Carpathians. Even today, peasants insist not only that their relatives or acquaintances have seen this or that supernatural being, but that they themselves have encountered an *opyr* or *upyr* (vampire), a *nucnyk* (night spirit), a *bosurkun* (sorcerer) or a *bosur-kanja* (witch)'.[9]

This belief is no more apparent, however, than in the heart of the Carpathian Mountains, where Transylvanians talk of the *miase nopte* (night spirit), representing the bad spirits who makes it dangerous to be out at night, or the *mama padura* (forest mother), a type of wood fairy who helps children who have lost their way and represents the good spirits. Another evil spirit is the *dschuma*, who brings plague or illness to a village and can only be countered by hanging a red shirt at the entrance to the village. This shirt must be spun, woven and sewed in one night by seven women or the method will fail.[10] Of all the spirits, the *strigoi* is perhaps the most feared. After a person dies, *pomana*, a kind of funeral feast, are held after a fortnight, six weeks, and one year after death for a period of seven years (this is in some ways similar to the practice of disinterment discussed above). They should also be held again if the dead person appears in the dreams of a family member. If these traditions are not strictly adhered to then the soul can become trapped on earth and cannot find rest, and these spirits become the *strigoi*.[11] There are generally two types of vampire being or *strigoi* in Romanian folklore and these are the dead vampire (the reanimated corpse) and the live vampire (it is believed that people destined to become vampires after death have the ability to send out their spirit to meet with dead vampires). In different parts of the region there are often different names to represent these, for example in Transylvania *siscoi* is sometimes used for live vampires, and *varcolaci* and *pricolici* sometimes refer to dead vampires but sometimes to wolf-like beings that eat the moon. The Ruthenian word for vampire is *uper*, and in Bukovina *vidme* refers to a witch or a live vampire but never a dead vampire.[12] A term perhaps more familiar to the West, and used by Gerard to describe a dead vampire, is *nosferatu*, and although it is sometimes used to describe the Transylvanian vampire, *strigoi* is the much more accepted term.

The *varcolac* is perhaps as infamous a being in Romania as the vampire, and is generally described as being a wolf-like creature similar to the more familiar werewolf. They are usually accredited with eating the moon and the sun and causing eclipses, or biting the moon until it appears covered in blood (again, denoted by an eclipse, either partial or total) so to prevent

Dracula in wolf form in Francis Ford Coppola's film *Bram Stoker's Dracula*.

this, during an eclipse 'peasants in Valcea beat on fire shovels to frighten the *varcolac* away from the moon. In Puma they toll the church bells. Elsewhere they make noises with tongs, gridirons, and irons of all sorts, beat trays, and let off guns. Gipsies play on the fiddle and lute – anything to make a noise'.[13] The suggested origin of the *varcolac* is that they are the souls of unbaptized children or the children of unmarried parents; either way, they are children cursed by God. Harry Senn suggests that the werewolves of many countries, including Serbia, Bulgaria, Slovenia and Romania, can be seen to relate to the cycles of the sun and moon and to festivals relating to these, similar in ways to the seasonal cyclic beliefs from the prehistoric era. The symbolism of the wolf devouring the moon therefore represents the end of a cycle and the beginning of a new one.[14]

This symbolism and the meaning and origins of the wolf within Romanian culture shall be discussed shortly, but first it is necessary to consider how the relationship between the wolf and the Romanian villages is reflected. In a story from folklore it is said that there was in a village a man,

who driving home from church on Sunday with his wife, suddenly felt that the time for his transformation had come. He therefore gave over the reins to her, and stepped aside into the bushes, where, murmuring the mystic formula, he turned three somersaults over a ditch. Soon after this the woman, waiting in vain for her husband, was attacked by a furious dog, which rushed, barking, out of the bushes and succeeded in biting her severely, as well as tearing her dress. When, an hour later, this woman reached home alone she was met by her husband, who advanced smiling to meet her, but between his teeth she caught signs of the shreds of her dress which had been bitten out by the dog, and the horror of the discovery caused her to faint away.[15]

There are many tales such as this from Romanian folklore that stipulate the fear and dangers regarding the werewolf, and for as long as the wolf is an integral part of Romania's wildlife, this fear of his supernatural cousin shall most likely remain.

Werewolves, vampires and so forth within Romanian folklore are found in a number of legends and oral traditions passed on through each generation, making tracing their origins somewhat problematic. These legends, however, play a big part in Romanian culture, which is littered with examples of werewolves, devils, witches and monstrous creatures. Whilst the origins of some legends are difficult to trace, others have more apparent sources such as the following curses that are linked to restrictions stipulated by the Church: 'Christian holidays are likewise the focus of sexual restrictions inscribed in the Church canon; that is, one must observe abstinence from sexual relations on the eve of Christmas, Easter and the Pentecost'. If these rules are not obeyed and a child is conceived, the child 'will be cursed with 'wolf-ears', for example, or a 'wolf's head,' or will have a harelip, and generally will be 'unlucky' and even 'malicious'.[16]

It is also possible that these legends, and in particular those regarding the wolf, stem from extremely early pre-Christian 'mystery religions',[17] such as those of Bacchus or Cybele. From a modern Romanian perspective the rituals or parades are a positive Christian act rather than a return to the pagan religions of old. Young, single males 'parade through Eastern European villages singing ritual hymns [called *colinde*] and performing dances, accompanied by musicians and others wearing animal masks . . . [festivals are] celebrated in Romania with masquerading, mumming and folk dramas using masks that represent animals, old people, and devils, in addition to animal costumes'.[18] These parades are evident in many Eastern European countries, and especially areas of Romania including Transylvania, Moldavia, Wallachia and Bucovina. This animalistic revelry is also apparent in the pre-Christian feast of the *Lupercalia*, where again groups of young males dressed as wolves or goats paraded through the streets chasing young women and whipping them with leather thongs, an act deemed to inspire fertility. It is possible that these early religious festivals were the foundations for later werewolf legends and traditions such as that of the French *loup-garou*, the word itself reflecting etymological links with the *Lupercalia*.

An interesting parallel that has been raised concerns the festival of Candlemas (15 February) and the practice of eating pancakes to symbolize the eating of the old moon and its absence from the sky during the festival.[19] This mirrors the deed committed by the *varcolac*, as discussed above, but although this was initially seen as a werewolf or vampire it is generally depicted in modern traditions as being an unbaptised or abandoned child with a keen appetite (essentially a type of wood spirit or nymph). February itself has long held traditions of celebrating the dead; the Roman Parentalia / Feralia or the remembrance of the dead, the final day of the Greek Anthesteria and the Babylonian feast of all souls were all celebrated in February,[20] but in modern times these celebrations have switched to the end of October / early November, particularly in Europe and America, culminating in

Halloween. It is interesting that the same werewolf, vampire, devil and monster masks and outfits are still donned, reflecting age-old traditions, and although in the West Halloween is largely a marketing ploy to encourage this behaviour, in parts of the world, for instance Eastern European countries, including Romania, they have infinitely more meaning and relevance.

St George's Day (23 April / 6 May on the Gregorian calendar) in Romania is another such occasion steeped in tradition and superstition; one must beware of witches on that day, but it is also a good day to find treasure, such as ancient earthenware jars filled with Dacian coins, according to legend.[21] In reality these 'treasures' were actually Roman offerings or coin hordes, but fuelled local superstitions, as it is believed that on St George's Day the treasure burned and gave off a bluish flame (an event witnessed at the beginning of *Dracula*). Also notable is the feast of St Elias (20 July / 1 August); it is said that if lightning were to strike a house on this day and cause it to catch fire, one must not extinguish it, as God himself has lit the fire. In some areas, however, extinguishing the fire is permitted but only if this is done using milk.[22] It was said that the inhabitants of one village witnessed the image of the Virgin Mary and of Christ 'miraculously' appearing on wooden objects such as walls and signposts. The ethnologist and anthropologist Petr Bogatyrev visited this village and was shown some of this imagery – rather proudly – by one of the peasants.[23] He admits that, to his eye, he could see nothing but some patterning amongst the wood, but the peasant would not be dissuaded. Although deemed to be miracles by the villagers, the clergy dismissed these claims and remonstrated with the villagers that there were no images; their response was that obviously the 'miracles' only revealed themselves to the peasants and so could not be seen by the clergy.

Other episodes detailed in Bogatyrev's accounts of his time spent in the Carpathians note a number of dreams or hallucinations relating to the return of loved ones from the dead, and particularly the story of one peasant woman who related her experience of being visited by her recently deceased mother and being choked by her in her sleep. This may have been rather the woman's emotions and grief for her dead mother than an actual vampiric visit 'from beyond the grave'. Therefore, it could be supposed that the vampire, in whatever guise, is a direct result of psychological occurrences. The image of the vampire today, for example, with his cape and fangs, is relative to the imagery that we have been constantly exposed to, through literature and filmography, for the past two hundred years. This in turn was an evolution of the vampire reports of the academics before them, and were created with these early ideas within their subconscious thought. Bogatyrev explains that 'psychologists have shown that everyone who describes one of his own dreams modifies it under the influence of similar dreams or phenomena he has heard. Likewise, the person who recounts how one spirit or another looked unconsciously modifies his vision during the course of his account under the influence of accounts of the same genre that he happened to hear previously'.[24]

Within folklore, one would expect that the different beings, such as the Devil or a vampire, should be viewed as separate entities, but quite often we find that this is not the case. This could be down to the notion that a peasant may find it difficult to imagine the Devil (in spirit form) existing without a 'solid' presence, possibly an animal, reanimated corpse or other such host.[25] Also, within folklore, vampires tend to be born rather than made, unlike the examples from vampire literature; those that are spirits or reanimated corpses are usually only seen at night, whereas those that are in witch or wizard form can exist at night or in daylight, which is perhaps why it tends to be the former entity that is adopted within literature. In Transylvanian vampire folklore it is said that these witches and vampires like to ride on hemp brakes or shovels if these items are left lying about, and this may be a possible origin for the image of witches riding on broomsticks in Western European traditions. It is also believed that these different types of vampires, be they the dead or live type, often meet at crossroads, churchyards, ruined houses or in the forest,[26] and again these are all places associated with vampire tales in the West, most especially the churchyard.

It is with Bogatyrev's theory in mind that we must now look to folkloric stories themselves. In one story from *Ion Creanga*[27] we hear how in Amărăşti, a rural village in central Romania, an old woman died. After several months the children of her eldest son begin to die, and then those of her youngest son. The sons go to their mother's grave, dig up her body, cut her in half and re-bury her. Still the deaths continue. Once more they dig up her body and are horrified to find it whole again, so they take the body into the forest, where they cut out her heart and burn it, mix the ashes with water and give the liquid to their remaining children to drink. After this, the deaths cease. Another story describes how in the nearby town of Văgíuleşti a certain peasant's children began to die one by one. The villagers hold council and decide that it is necessary to take a white horse to the village graveyard in order to determine if any vampires are present. The horse jumps over all the graves until it gets to that of the peasant's mother-in-law, who it is said had been a witch in life. The horse refuses to pass over the grave, snorting and neighing and stamping its hoof. That night, the peasant and his son go to the grave and dig up the woman's body, which they find sitting up, with long hair and fingernails, and with her skin all red. They cover the body in straw and shavings, pour wine over it and set it ablaze, after which they rebury it and return home.[28] It is not mentioned whether this puts an end to the deaths, but one must assume that it does, for there is no further account of any such occurrence.

A further story from Botoşani in the north-east tells of a young man and woman in love. The young man dies and becomes a vampire but cannot enter the girl's house as it is 'clean and holy', so he invites her to go with him to his tomb. Once there, the girl makes the excuse that she cannot enter as she has lost her beads and must find them, and then proceeds to run away from the vampire. She notices a house with a light on and enters, where she finds a dead man slumped on the table. The girl hides as the vampire furiously knocks on the door and demands the man open it; as the dead man rises from the table the girl realizes he is a vampire also, but just as she feels she is doomed, the cock crows for dawn and the vampires are thwarted. The moral of the story is that the girl escaped because she was clean and holy, and vampires struggle to catch clean souls.[29]

Another vampire story from Siret in northern Romania is markedly different to the previous examples, as it describes how the vampire wandered from village to village killing the inhabitants. As he is about to embark on another spree he decides to bake some bread for the journey (it is interesting to note that the vampire can eat normal food as in Western literature they cannot, preferring instead to diet on blood), and as he is doing this some workmen pass by and decide to call in to light their pipes. Just as they enter, the vampire instantly becomes a cat, so, on seeing there is no-one at home, the workmen help themselves to the bread, leaving only one loaf for the cat to eat. When the workmen leave, the vampire visits the surrounding villages, taking the loaf of bread with him, and attacks all the people there and tears them to pieces. Once more, the workmen call at the house on their way home, but this time the vampire meets them and informs them of his deeds, telling them if they had not left the single loaf of bread behind they would have been instantly bewitched and all would have died.[30]

A final example, also from Siret, details how some returning soldiers are offered a lift by an old man on his cart. As they travel through Transylvania, where the man was attempting to buy some hay, they stop at a house where a woman invites them in and gives them a meal of porridge and milk, before leaving them to eat in peace. After the meal, the soldiers look for the woman to thank her but cannot find her anywhere. On climbing into the attic, they are horrified to discover the bodies of seven people, one of which is the woman who made them the food. The soldiers flee in fright, but as they do so they see seven lights descending on the house – the souls of the vampire bodies! The story narrates how, if the soldiers had turned the bodies over so they were facing downwards, the souls would not have been able to re-renter the bodies.[31]

It is apparent that stories of vampires within Romanian folk-lore differ from example to example and this is also the case in the suggested causes of how people become vampires. Although, as mentioned, one vampire cannot 'create' another vampire, the majority of vampires are predetermined, in that it is usually the case that a person's actions in life cause them to become a vampire after death. For example, if a person lives a bad life, if a man falsely obtains money or a woman uses spells or incantations (effectively, if she is a witch), they may become vampires. There are also natural reasons for a person becoming a vampire, for example, if they are born with a caul (this person would become a vampire six weeks after death) or if a child dies before being baptised. Among the most curious reasons for becoming a vampire are: if a man does not eat garlic, if a pregnant woman does not eat salt or if a vampire casts his eye upon a pregnant woman (then the baby will become a vampire). If there are seven children of the same sex in a family then the seventh is cursed to become a vampire, or if a cat jumps over or a person's shadow falls over a corpse, this too causes vampirism.[32]

Once a person is a vampire, and if its evil ways are not stopped, it will continue for a period of seven years, during which it will first kill its relations, then the other residents and animals of its village, then those of every village in its country, after which it will pass into another country where a different language is spoken. There it will become a man again.[33] Once the man marries and has children and they in turn die, they will also become vampires and the process starts once more. To prevent this from happening, then, the vampire must be destroyed, thus ending his evil trail of death. Again, there are many suggestions on how this should be done. The most common worldwide idea of how to destroy a vampire is to put a stake through its heart. In Bulgaria, though, it should be a red-hot iron that is used rather than a stake and in Valcea, as mentioned earlier concerning the death's-head moths, a needle is deemed sufficient. In Romania, however, the traditional method is to exhume the body on a Saturday, then drive a stake through the navel or cut out the heart. The heart should then be burned, with the ashes collected, or boiled and then cut into pieces. These are sometimes thrown into a river, but are usually mixed with water to give to sick people or the vampire's relatives, or sometimes used to anoint people or animals to protect them from evil spirits.[34]

Other methods include laying the body face down in the grave so it cannot rise, placing items in the mouth such as pebbles, garlic or incense for the vampire to gnaw, or filling the coffin with millet grains or seeds for the vampire to count, all of which delay the vampire rather than destroy it. Garlic is widely known throughout history for its health benefits, but within Romania it is further accepted that it has powers to ward off evil spirits, vampires and wolves, and on particular days of the year when it is thought evil spirits are abroad, garlic is rubbed on windows in the pattern of a cross, placed above the door or rubbed on all means of entry to a building, and sometimes even rubbed on farm animals to protect them against vampires.[35]

A final example of vampires within traditional folklore is from the area of Mihalcea, where it is believed that certain types of vampires, particularly those of the live sort and only those that are female, have the ability to drain things of their power. For example, some can take the power of other women, of animals such as hens or bees (resulting in the bees no longer being able to collect honey), of the elements such as the wind or rain, or even of bread.[36] This is certainly a curious suggestion, but one that holds obvious parallels with modern so-called 'psychic vampires' who drain the energy of other people. This could well be the origin in the West for the idea of draining the life-force of a person through the consumption of their blood.

Today it is fair to say that the traditional idea of the vampire in modern Transylvania, and indeed in wider Romania and Eastern Europe as a whole, has lost its relevance somewhat, leaving in its wake the commercialized 'tourist vampire' readily marketed to the West. This may well be down to Romania's attempt to shake off its superstitious and backward image as it moves into the European Union, and particularly the shackles of Communism post-Ceauşescu, but also to promote the idea of it being a country steeped in tourism and culture, something which is necessary if it is to mature within the twenty-first century. This tourism factor is no more apparent than in the purely ridiculous proposal of building a Dracula theme park in Transylvania.[37] The spectacular landscape, conflicting architecture and industrious peoples of Romania converge to make the region a jewel in Eastern Europe, something that a 'vampiric Disneyland' would utterly destroy.[38] How this level of modernization would affect Romania's natural beauty draws parallels with Ceauşescu's urbanization project, which saw endless rural villages destroyed and the inhabitants moved into identical concrete blocks, leaving little scope for imagination or individuality, and attempting to crush the country's spirit. Brasov, Transylvania's capital in the south, is an excellent example of this. Entering from the south on the main route from Bucharest, one arrives at a concrete metropolis, full of drab and cheerless uniform buildings and industries. The 'old town', in the northern section of Brasov, is worlds apart from this with its perfect mix of medieval fortifications and churches, German-baroque hybrid architecture and its neat

Bran Castle.

Strada Republicii, a cosmopolitan blend of fashion outlets, bars and coffee houses – and this is the heart of Dracula country? On visiting, one marvels at the diverse inhabitants; only here would elderly peasants in layer upon layer of threadbare, dirty clothing be comfortable walking alongside the urban chic of Romania's youth, complete with garish designer clothes and sunglasses.

This is not to suggest that the idea of the vampire has disappeared entirely within Romania, and in the isolated rural villages of Romania's countryside vampire superstition and fear is still as strong as ever. Yet it is the vampire tourist industry that has largely swept aside the traditional image. The most famous and widely visited of Romania's vampire tourist hotspots is

Bran Castle, in southern Transylvania, commonly described and marketed as being 'Dracula's Castle'.

Bran Castle was built in 1212 as a fortress of the Teutonic Knights and was originally a wooden structure, but was later reinforced in stone. After partial demolition by the Turks in 1377, King Louis of Hungary gave permission for the Saxon inhabitants of Kronstadt (Brasov) to build the current castle there. It was then used as a defensive outpost in the continuing struggles against the Turks, by Mircea the Great (Vlad Dracula's grandfather) among others, but was eventually given over to the Romanian royal family in 1920, whereupon Queen Marie, a granddaughter of Queen Victoria of Britain, made it her residence. Her daughter, Princess Ileanu, inherited the castle after Queen Marie's death until the Communist regime took it over in 1948. It was returned to Princess Ileanu's son, Dominic von Habsburg, by the Romanian government in 2006, who promptly put Castle Bran up for sale in 2007 at a cost of US$78 million (approx. £40 million), where it was advertised as being 'Dracula's Castle'.

The castle itself is a fine example of mixed Gothic and Renaissance architecture and could indeed be mistaken for a vampire's lair but, sadly, the only vampires present are those adorning the many T-shirts, mugs and novelty gifts being peddled on the stalls outside the entrance to the grounds. Indeed, as I approached Bran from nearby Brasov the Romanian taxi driver piped up in broken English 'Ah! Bran Castle! It is wonderful. Do not expect any vampires though . . . this is just legend! A good legend, we make a lot of money from it'. The village of Bran also lends itself quite well to the vampire legend; its rows of wooden houses, huge piles of logs and haystacks and animals roaming free in abundance reflect the traditional image of the Eastern European village and whilst being a testament to Romania's poor, rural areas, is a stark contrast to the multi-million pound castle above.

The entrance to Bran Castle.

The castle itself looms ominously from its seat atop a craggy outcrop looking for all the world like the home of that most famous of vampires. A flight of steep steps leads to a large, wooden door remarkably akin to the many examples from vampire cinema, which one half expects to creak open and reveal

Count Dracula himself. Alas, it is not to be, and here the similarities with Dracula's Castle end. Once inside, the air of the dark, foreboding castle immediately turns to one of pleasant welcome with its polished wooden floors and whitewashed walls creating a canvas on which many fine examples of Romanian, German and Austrian furniture are displayed. For Bran Castle today is a museum to Romania's royal past, and houses some truly remarkable pieces of Transylvania's history, from the pictures, tapestries, furnishings and armoury to the examples of traditional Transylvanian peasant houses on display in the castle grounds.

As regards Bram Stoker's novel, Count Dracula's castle was set some considerable distance north on the Borgo Pass near Bistritz and to what extent, if any, this was influenced by Bran remains open to debate. As far as Vlad Dracula is concerned, there are suggestions that he may have stayed there on one of his many visits to Transylvania or that he may have been imprisoned there for a short time in 1462. But here, again, the links with vampires end. Arriving at Bran one is struck by the anticipation of entering a 'vampire's castle' but one leaves with a feeling of anti-climax. You know it could not possibly have been a *real* vampire's home, but after all the marketing regarding Bran and vampires, one might have expected at least one portrait whose eyes followed you around the room! And so to the real Castle Dracula, the fortress of Poienari, high on top of the Wallachian mountains above the River Argeş.

The discovery of Poienari as the real Castle Dracula was made through the research of vampirologists Raymond McNally and Radu Florescu in the 1960s. They were looking, however, for the fictional Dracula's real castle rather than the real Dracula's fictional castle. That is, the home of Bram Stoker's vampire count, rather than the Wallachian Prince Vlad. Attempts to trace the castle that Stoker had based his castle on ranged too far north, but this was not surprising as Stoker had never been to Transylvania and was basing his geography on books and maps.

So McNally and Florescu's research led them considerably further south towards Curtea de Argeş and eventually Poienari Castle:

> High up in the Transylvanian Alps we came to a halt. There, atop a black volcanic rock formation, bordering the Arges River and framed by a massive alpine snow-capped landscape, lay the twisted battlements of Castle Dracula, its remains barely distinguishable from the rock of the mountain itself.[39]

Indeed, to reach Poienari one must climb over 1,400 steps and brave the terrifying drops to cross a short, narrow bridge before climbing a final flight of stairs and entering the ruins themselves. Part of the fortress collapsed in 1888 (interestingly, at the same time Stoker was researching and writing Dracula), sending the stone tumbling down into the valley below; legend suggests that Vlad's wife was herself plummeting to her death when the fortress collapsed (see chapter Five).

On our climb to the summit we met not a single other person, despite the suggestion that Poienari is a tourist hotspot, and this is undoubtedly down to the fact that a great deal of determination is needed, not to mention an exceptional head for heights, and also that Poienari is not a fraction as marketable as Bran is as it is in ruins, despite it actually being the real Castle Dracula. Once in the ruins of the castle, the atmosphere is one of peace and tranquility, and the vantage point offers stunning views of the surrounding region, no doubt offering Vlad an excellent base from which to scheme and survey.

Legend has it that during a festival on Easter Day at Târgovişte, Vlad's capital of Wallachia, many of the inhabitants were rejoicing amongst the revelry, dressed in their finest garb. It was during the period after Constantinople had fallen to the Turks (1453) and when Vlad had discovered his brother Mircea

The Chindia Tower.

had been murdered by his boyars (see chapter Five). Vlad ordered the 500 traitorous boyars and their families to be taken captive and then, overlooking the proceedings from his Chindia watchtower, had many of them impaled. The remaining ones were shackled and marched to the site of Poienari where they were forced to build the fortress until 'their clothes fell from their backs'. A story from Romanian folklore, *The Fortress of Poienari*, details how

> Masons, stonecutters, carpenters, blacksmiths, all those who knew any trade, set to work. Those who hitherto

Vlad Dracula's princely court, Târgoviște, Romania.

had been brought up in luxury, mixed mortar, women chipped stones, young girls carried water, and even children were set to work suitable for their age. One might see at the top and the sides of the mountain, a human ant-hill, always in motion, occupied in this atrocious labour.[40]

When completed it had double reinforced walls, five cylindrical towers, a well with its own water supply and an escape tunnel.[41] Today one can only imagine Poienari at its climax, protecting Vlad and his men from numerous assaults by the Turks. It is said that when the Turks finally overcame Vlad's forces at Poienari, firing their guns from the adjacent mountain, Vlad and his men escaped the fortress via the secret tunnel and fooled the Turks by shoeing their horses back to front, thus leaving tracks facing the wrong direction and avoiding capture. In the

Ariel view of the princely court.

end it was not the Turkish bombardment that finally brought Poienari down, however, but a series of earthquakes, leaving the ruined shell that remains today.

Returning to Târgoviște, the most well-preserved remains from Dracula's rule are those of his princely court and the recently restored Chindia tower. Wandering through the ruins of the Palace, one cannot but reflect on the legends of Dracula and the many people who were impaled in the courtyard. Climbing the tower, which was restored in the nineteenth century and now houses a small museum devoted to Dracula, one has a spectacular view of the remains and the princely church (added in the sixteenth century), which houses some marvellously painted frescoes depicting some of the Wallachian rulers such as Basarab and Brancoveanu. In the entranceway to the complex is a wall plaque listing the forty *voivodes* (leaders or princes) of Wallachia, including Mircea, Vlad Dracul and

Dracula himself. It is perhaps fitting, then, that while being the principal residence of the man deemed a bloodthirsty tyrant, Târgovişte is also the place where the other infamous Romanian tyrant, Nicolae Ceauşescu, finally met his death by firing squad on Christmas Day 1989. But who exactly was Vlad, the man known to history as the real Dracula?

# FIVE

# The Historical Dracula: Vlad III Ţepeş

Your soul is black like hell,
It makes even bloody Satan wonder,
Your thoughts are dark,
They cannot see your evils,
Like blind night groping in darkness,
With no star on the firmament
Vasile Alecsandri, *Legende*

The view of many historians on the character and deeds of Vlad III (known as Ţepeş, The Impaler or Dracula) is of a cruel and bloodthirsty tyrant who tortured and murdered thousands of his enemies and fellow countrymen alike. Yet the truth behind the real Dracula is a complex one, and this evil image portrayed for so long is not necessarily the whole picture. He is one of those figures who could well have been lost to history were it not for two important events. The most recent (and most important from an Eastern perspective) was the Romanian Dictator Nicolae Ceauşescu's adoption of Vlad as a national hero, issuing a commemorative stamp in 1976 to mark the 500th anniversary of Vlad's death. The other event, and one that is recognized the world over, is Bram Stoker's use of Vlad's nickname 'Dracula' for his famous vampire count.[1] Vlad's father was known as Vlad Dracul, meaning dragon. He was a member of the 'Order of the Dragon', a chivalric society set up by King Sigismund of Hungary to defend Christendom against the Turks. The suffix 'ulya' simply means 'son of' in Wallachia (now in modern-day Romania). Dracula, or Drakulya, would therefore mean 'son of the dragon'. *Dracul* also means

A 15th-century portrait of Vlad the Impaler from Castle Ambras, Austria.

'devil' in Romanian, so some think Dracula means 'son of the Devil'.

Many people do not realize that there actually was a real-life 'Dracula', a person as bloodthirsty as his fictional counterpart, but certainly not a vampire. What this creates is a 'split personality' for Vlad: in the West he is seen as a cruel and bloodthirsty tyrant with strong vampire connections (recently depicted in Francis Ford Coppola's film adaptation of *Bram Stoker's Dracula* and Elizabeth Kostova's novel, *The Historian*, wherein the vampire Dracula and Vlad Dracula are one and the same), while in the East he is regarded as a national hero who defended his country from Turkish oppressors and who has no vampire connections whatsoever.

Are there any actual links between the historical Dracula and vampires? It is true that comparisons can be made between the events and actions of Vlad's life and certain aspects of vampire lore. Before these can be considered, it is important to examine the events that shaped Vlad's personality and the contemporary documentary evidence, such as the German and Russian pamphlets and Romanian oral tales, that has created the bloodthirsty image we have of him today.

Dracula was born in Sighisoara in Transylvania in 1436, son of the then Prince of Wallachia Vlad II Dracul. He ruled as Prince himself on three occasions (1448, 1456–62 and 1476) before his death at the end of 1476, something that again throws up its own mysteries and intrigue. Although a detailed biography of Vlad's life is not necessary here,[2] I will discuss certain events that, I will argue, were directly responsible for the anger, cruelty and distrust evident in Vlad Dracula's character. It may be that the death of Vlad's father was the catalyst for the animosity and suspicion shown toward others by him in later life. The ultimate betrayal of Vlad II Dracul by his boyars (nobles), which led to his death in 1447, was something that obviously affected Vlad III Dracula deeply, as his later reforms and punishments hit traitors hard. Disloyalty, violence and treason were rife amongst the corrupt boyars at the time of Dracula's ascension; 'truth is hushed up, gone is all decency, the reins of law are slack . . . the iron will and uncontrollable violence kill, disregarding everybody's rights; hatred, treason and the bitterest oppression are at ease', as Bishop Ioan of Zredna informs us.

The exact date and place of Vlad II Dracul's murder is not clear, but it most likely occurred in November or December 1447 at the village of Balteni. The main perpetrator of his murder was János Hunyadi (Iancu of Hunedoara in Romanian), King of Hungary, the man also responsible for the murder of Dracula's older brother Mircea, who had been Prince of Wallachia himself during his father's campaigns away. Mircea was also murdered the same year (Dracula later discovered that Mircea had been buried alive). Up until this point Dracula and his younger brother Radu had been political captives of the Turks at Ezirne, but on the death of their father they were released. Radu committed the ultimate act of treason to his native Wallachia and opted to join the Turks. This act of betrayal completed the three betrayals that had killed Dracula's family: his father and older brother were dead; and his younger brother had abandoned him for the enemy. What this must have done to Dracula psychologically can only be imagined, but to someone as passionate and patriotic as he was, the memory of betrayal must have stayed with him for the rest of his life.

After a brief spell as Voivod of Wallachia (October–November 1448), Dracula sought refuge with his uncle Bogdan and cousin Stephen the Great in Moldavia, but Bogdan too was murdered in 1451. The growing threat of Turkish invasion from the Ottoman sultan Mehmet II led to an unlikely allegiance between Dracula and the Hungarian statesman Janos Hunyadi, with Dracula being given guardianship of the Transylvanian borders. It was a clever move politically, and Dracula was able to put his personal feelings aside in order to progress. With Transylvanian support he was able to become Voivod of Wallachia for a second time in 1456 after the death of the current ruler Vladislav II. That same year Janos Hunyadi died, and Dracula made a peace treaty with the new King of Hungary, Ladislaus, thus ensuring a stable foundation from which to rule and protect his country from the ever-growing threat of the Turks. What is apparent from all this is that the period was extremely turbulent and unpredictable, with treachery and betrayal rife. What Dracula sought to do during his six-year reign was eradicate this and create a country which was safe, fair and above all united, and it was in this period that Dracula's reputation and the image that survives of him was created.

Vlad the Impaler eating among impaled bodies, 15th-century German woodcut.

There are numerous 'anecdotes' of Dracula's actions against his enemies (be these foreign invaders, corrupt merchants, traitorous boyars or the lazy, sick and poor) as well as famous woodcuts depicting his cruel methods, such as *The Feast of the Impaled*, showing Dracula dining among impaled corpses,[3] reproduced in many surviving contemporary manuscripts. These manuscripts do not always agree with each other; sometimes there are subtle differences in the details. Often the deeds they record are written from a certain point of view, be it compassionate and understanding or in shock and in horror of Dracula's actions.

Before we discuss in detail the various motives, aims and consequences of the anecdotes it is important to note that although certain ones are evidently biased (such as the German ones, due to Dracula's persecution of the Saxon merchants) they all conform to and document certain characteristic traits and methods widely known to relate to Dracula. Of these, none is more notorious than his infamous torture methods, particularly impalement. Dracula is in fact more well-known as Vlad the Impaler (Țepeș in Romanian) than as Vlad Dracula, and impalement is often associated exclusively with Vlad. There are varying suggestions on the method of impalement, but the most common way was to pin down or fasten the victim to the ground and attach a rope to each leg. These ropes could then be attached to a horse, for example, or be pulled by one or two other people. A sharpened stake is then inserted into the anus of the victim and their body forcibly pulled onto the stake by the ropes attached to the legs. The stake would then be hoisted up and inserted into the ground, leaving the victim trapped on the stake. Over time (perhaps several hours or sometimes days)

Method of impalement (1).

the body would slowly slip further onto the stake with the sharpened end working its way up through the abdominal region, into the chest and eventually puncturing through the chest, or exiting via the throat or mouth. This method reflects a sadistic wish to inflict pain and suffering before death.

Dracula did not invent impalement however, far from it, and there is a debate as to how he discovered this method of torture. The most likely explanation is that he witnessed an act of impalement while being held prisoner by the Turks,[4] as impalement is evidenced in Turkish culture: 'Why soot your hands if you don't want to forge? Why this meeting if you're afraid to speak? Once you escaped the Turkish impalement; you should've rotted on their gallows instead!',[5] but this itself must draw on earlier examples such as those of the Ancient Greeks, Persians and Egyptians. The Greek historian Herodotus, in *The History of Herodotus*, mentions this punishment used by King Xerxes on Sataspes, son of Teaspes the Achaemenian, as he had 'failed to accomplish the task set him [he] was impaled by the king's orders in accordance with the former sentence'.[6]

Method of impalement (2).

83

Although it is the most infamous of Dracula's torture methods, impalement was not the only one he used. There are examples of his victims being boiled alive, flayed, having limbs cut off and mothers having their breasts hacked off and their babies impaled; there is even the suggestion that Dracula may have used 'germ warfare', as he reputedly paid Wallachians infected with diseases such as syphilis or tuberculosis to dress as Ottomans and enter the enemy camps, thus spreading disease to the Turks. (The problem with this latter technique is that infecting large enough numbers to have made a noticeable difference would have taken a long time, possibly up to twenty years with syphilis, and any more debilitating diseases such as leprosy would have been noticeable, so the victims would have been quarantined straight away.[7])

There could be any number of reasons why Dracula adopted his barbaric tactics and many of these relate to a pragmatic, if overtly extreme, response. Theses factors could include revenge (against the traitorous boyars), inter-family feuds (between the rival Draculeşti and Daneşti families), protection of commerce (relating to Transylvania / Saxon merchants), personal authority (reinforcing and stabilizing his newly gained position as Voivod) and national sovereignty (a factor deemed highly important to Dracula).[8] Whether the atrocities themselves are in fact real or not is less important than the symbolism within them: that Dracula would punish the wrong-doer and reward the good. One such story relates how some visiting Turkish emissaries were brought before Dracula, whereupon they declined to remove their turbans, explaining that in their culture this was never done. This presumed lack of respect infuriated Dracula, who had the turbans nailed to their heads in order to 'consolidate their culture'. Another such tale, taken from the Romanian point of view, involved two monks, one a 'crafty Greek monk' the other a 'poor Romanian priest'. Both were brought before Dracula, who asked them separately 'on their travels how had his people described him?'. The Greek monk replied that everyone praised him and spoke highly of his name, but that he should be kinder to his supporters from holy places and give them financial aid. Dracula then asked the Romanian priest the same question and received the response that some were beginning to lose faith in him and that they believed he no longer lessened their burdens. Dracula praised the Romanian for his honesty and let him go, but ordered that the Greek monk be impaled for his lies, branding him an unworthy villain.[9]

There are clear underlying messages here, especially as the Romanian version is from a set of folk tales that suggest that the Romanian peoples honestly believe Dracula to have been a fair and just, if strict, ruler. Other versions of the stories adopt an entirely different perspective. The German stories tend to reflect a propagandistic viewpoint, accusing Dracula of being like other persecutors of Christendom, such as Herod, Nero and Diocletian.[10] It is useful at this point to note that the Wallachia that Dracula inherited in 1456, which had a population of around half a million, was largely comprised of four sections of society: the boyars, the church, the peasants and a middle-class of tradesmen and craftsmen (the Saxons). The main reason for the portrayal of Dracula in Saxon and Germanic accounts as a bloodthirsty fiend, for example, in contemporary pamphlets from Nuremberg, was his barbarity toward these Saxon merchants, who he believed had been 'bleeding his country dry'.[11] This is a fair suggestion, to an extent, as the Saxon merchants had been able to monopolize the commerce and trade markets and the corrupt boyars did little to rectify this. However, the main point that can be gleaned from the manuscripts is that it was not a person's status, ethnicity or value (be they a priest, lord or peasant) that determined their worth and treatment in Dracula's mind but their moral code of conduct; if they were honest and just they would live; if immoral, corrupt or traitorous they would die.

There are exceptions to this code, however, particularly evident in the 'Burning of the Poor'. The German stories describe this episode thus: 'He also had the poor people who were in his land invited to his house; after they had eaten there, he had them all burned in a small building. There were two hundred of them'.[12] A rather abrupt explanation, and one that merely relates Dracula's atrocity rather than attempting to explain it, perhaps suggesting that with Dracula's actions there were no explanations and he was merely a cruel tyrant. The Romanian version, however, offers more detail. It states that during Dracula's reign there were many people who were out of work and could not afford any food, and so wandered aimlessly, begging without working, although many were fit enough to work. The story states that 'the Gospel says that man shall earn his daily bread only through the sweat of his brow'[13] on which Dracula reflected that these itinerant beggars lived off the sweat of others, so were useless to society and were in effect no better than thieves. He thus invited all the beggars to his capital at Targoviste and laid on a great feast for them in his hall. When they had eaten and drunk their fill, Dracula ordered the building to be locked and set ablaze. The story ends with poignant sarcasm: 'And do you believe that the breed of poor was wiped out? Far from it . . . even today times are not better than they were then. Beggars will cease to exist only with the end of the world'.[14]

Let us now consider how accurately we deem Dracula and his actions to have been portrayed within the documentary evidence. Taking the example of the emissary from Matthias Corvinus, the Hungarian king, we hear in the Russian account of events[15] that when Dracula received him he had a gilded stake set up before the emissary, and proceeded to enquire of him why he thought Dracula had done this. The emissary's response was that 'some nobleman [has obviously] committed a crime against you and you want to reserve a more honourable death for him than the others',[16] to which Dracula announced

that the stake was indeed for him. The emissary replied that if
he had committed a crime worthy of death then Dracula could
punish him as he saw fit, for he was a fair ruler and harboured
no guilt towards his death, the blame lying with no-one but
himself. On hearing this, Dracula allowed him to live and hon-
oured him greatly. This situation is again symbolic: if a person
is honest, humble and good they would not only be spared by
Dracula, but rewarded also. Surely, faced with a certain and
painful death, it is highly unlikely that this report of the emissary's response is accurate? One wonders how much the origin
of these existing stories owes to morality tales, cleverly combined with existing fables and folk tales of a man deemed by
the 'simple people'[17] to be a national hero. At the archive at
Sibiu, Transylvania, a German manuscript bears the signature
'Drakulya',[18] suggesting not only the authenticity of the docu-

ment but also first-hand evidence that Dracula was indeed using his nickname, whatever its meaning. On the other hand, when considering the 1456 treaty between Dracula and Ladislaus, King of Hungary, we hear that 'had Țepeș been enthroned by the Turks, why should he have been afraid to be ousted by those very Turks, in the very first year, in the very first months of his rule?'.[19] The documentary evidence on how accurate the tales of Dracula were is often far from conclusive.

For example, one might consider the conflicting accounts of the events of the infamous 'night attack' on the evening of 17 June 1462, which caused a considerable casualty rate for the Ottoman army. Here we shall witness the contradiction and fabrication apparent among the differing versions:

> Dracula carried out an incredible massacre without losing many men . . . the Sultan lost all confidence in the situation. During the night [he] abandoned the camp and fled in a shameful manner . . . [he was] reprimanded by his friends and brought back, almost against his will.[20]

> [The Wallachians] first encountered the army from Anatolia and they read verses of welcome and death to them, as they deserved . . . most of them were wounded or killed when they were trying to run away. Their defeat was so great that even ten-year-old children who were apprentices and servants in the army killed many Infidels twice as powerful as themselves.[21]

It would appear that these two accounts are describing two separate battles, although they are both, indeed, describing the 'night attack', and are perhaps the best example within the manuscripts of how a certain bias can grotesquely twist the actual events into historical propaganda. It is possible that the exact origin of the pamphlets and manuscripts relate to the account of the Benedictine monk Brother Jacob, whose narrative of the atrocities committed by Dracula on one of his fellow monks is the oldest surviving documentation.[22]

Whether the accounts of the various manuscripts are accurate or not, one assumes that there is an element of truth to them. And yet the debate on the validity and meaning of the content continues. Attitudes towards Dracula and his actions still cloud people's judgement as much now as they did in Dracula's time. Take the instance of Dracula's impalement of the Brasov boyars for example; Eastern, pro-Dracula historians suggest that the reason was ostensibly down to the boyars' failure to recognize the seven rulers of the Draculeşti / Daneşti families, but was really an act to consolidate Dracula's power and deter treachery.[23] Later theories[24] tend to suggest that the boyars were killed due to their obvious disloyalty and lack of support for the many rulers of Wallachia, which gives rise to the suggestion that their impalement was in part a revenge killing for both the death of Vlad Dracul and the greed and corruption that had allowed Dracula's beloved country to become weak and immoral. Killing them had the added bonus of stamping out the corruption, thus consolidating Dracula's power.

Dracula can therefore, partly because of his actions and partly because of the manuscripts' portrayal of them, be seen as either a tyrannical madman or a heroic protector who gave his life to defend his people from foreign invaders. The truth most likely lies somewhere in the middle. He undoubtedly committed many horrific acts, but in this he was not alone. Dracula lived in a world that was savage and brutal and one must question whether his deeds were any worse than the Inquisitor's torture methods, the barbarity shown by the Turks on prisoners or the torture that undoubtedly went on in almost every country throughout the medieval world.

Another suggestion, from Francis Ford Coppola's film *Bram Stoker's Dracula*, is that Dracula could have become a vampire through his conversion to Catholicism from the Orthodox Christian faith. In the film, Dracula's wife has died because she believed he had been killed in battle by the Turks and rather than live without him and surrender herself to them, she took her own life. While this is an addition by Coppola which does not appear in Bram Stoker's novel or research notes, there may be an element of truth. In the manuscripts there is a story that the Turks had surrounded Dracula's mountain fortress at Poienari and fired an arrow into the castle with a message relaying the false news of Dracula's death. This seems highly improbable as it would have to have been a remarkable shot to fire the arrow so high and with pinpoint accuracy, and is perhaps again an addition to the story to make it more interesting. It is interesting to note once more the link with suicide and vampirism, although there is no suggestion that Dracula's wife became a vampire.

In the film, Dracula renounces God (rather than converting to Catholicism) because of his apparent betrayal by him; he suggests that he is doing God's work by protecting his land against the Infidel, but God's thanks is to take his wife from him. In reality, Dracula converted to Catholicism, most likely for purely political reasons: '(Dracula) was raised probably as a Catholic, who converted to Islam, reconverted to the Orthodox Church and finally to Catholicism again . . . [this was] most likely seen to be taking realpolitik a little too far'.[25] Dracula played an extremely dangerous juggling game with his religion and his politics during his lifetime, but the focus of his final switch to Catholicism, and suggested vampirism as a consequence, does not take into account his earlier adoption of the Muslim faith while a political prisoner of the Turks. Surely this was more of a defiance of the Christian God? The accusation of vampirism because of his switch of faith seems a touch desperate, and is most likely another attempt to slur the name of Dracula by his enemies.

Poienari Castle, Arefu, near Curtea de Arges, Romania.

The closest link of vampirism with Dracula is the allegation of blood-drinking put forward, it is alleged, in Michael Beheim's fifteenth-century poem, 'A bloodthirsty tyrant named Dracula from Wallachia'. Beheim (1416–*c.* 1474) was the court poet of Holy Roman Emperor Frederick III (1415–1493), and is said to have been a *Minnesinger* or *Meistersinger*. His tale of Dracula was hugely popular at the time. It is one part of the story, however, that is of particular importance to the Dracula as vampire myth, according to McNally and Florescu: 'In one verse Beheim described Dracula as dipping his bread in the blood of his victims, which technically makes him a living vampire'.[26] Elizabeth Miller, President of the Canadian sector of the Transylvanian Society of Dracula, is only too quick to admit she fell into the trap of wholeheartedly believing McNally and Florescu's misleading statement: 'There was one document that said he (Dracula) used to dip bread into the blood of victims and eat the bread'.[27] She admitted that she later learned first hand of the gross misjudgement in this: 'I have a copy of the original Beheim manuscript [from Heidelberg]. Two German scholars have independently translated the appropriate stanza – and the rest of the poem. [They found] nothing'.[28]

The actual translation of the verse in question reads:

> It was his pleasure and gave him courage,
> To see human blood flow,
> [And] it was his custom to wash his hands in it,
> as it [or he] was brought to the dinner table.[29]

So Dracula *washed his hands* in the blood, not dipped his bread in it, if, indeed, this is a literal account of what happened. Often the metaphorical terms 'bathing in the blood of the enemy' or 'washing your hands in blood' (hence the phrase 'blood-bath') are applied to suggest some guilt or blame in a given situation usually involving the spilling of blood, and are not representative of *actual* washing or bathing in blood. Given Dracula's bloodthirsty (again, not indicative of the consumption of blood!) manner it would not be surprising if he did indeed wash his hands in the blood, but either way, this does not constitute an act of 'vampirism'. And this is the entire evidence concerning Dracula and blood-drinking found in the historical documentation. A curious point worthy of mention comes from the official tourist guide to Bran Castle, *Dracula: Myth or Reality*, in which there is a statement that reads 'an engraving of these narratives presents the prince [Dracula] in the middle of a . . . forest, waiting for his servants to bring him an unusual menu: human organs'.[30] This details the same occasion as Beheim's poem, 'The Feast of the Impaled', and probably utilizes Beheim's narrative itself, but makes no mention of the blood-drinking episode put forward by McNally and Florescu. Rather, it hints at a form of cannibalism, but is most likely again mere propaganda aimed at tourists. McNally and Florescu's assertion was hugely influential because they were instrumental in bringing both Dracula and the vampire connection within Romania into the forefront of historical debate; their claim has too often misled others into making false assumptions.

This leads us to the final point in question, which concerns Bram Stoker's *Dracula*. While the novel itself is considered in greater detail later, it is necessary to reflect briefly on two areas: the *actual* evidence linking the historical and fictional Draculas, and the *supposed* evidence.[31] Stoker set part of the story in Transylvania and adopted the name Dracula only at a very late date (originally it was set in Austria and the vampire was called Count Vampyre). This must therefore suggest that his vampire was not modelled, to any great extent, on Vlad Dracula. Obviously he used the name Dracula, but this was perhaps a more sinister sounding name and fitted in quite well with the geography of the story,[32] and he does briefly hint at certain parts of Dracula's history in the novel (these he does get wrong from time to time; for example, he has Count Dracula describing himself as a Szekler, which Vlad Dracula was not). On the subject of the name, and this is something that Stoker may or may not have been aware of, the term 'Dracula' was also adopted by Vlad Dracul's other sons Mircea and Radu cel Frumos (the Handsome), so did not exclusively refer to Vlad Țepeș. It may be that Stoker knew this and simply liked the name for his vampire, and was not intending to link his vampire exclusively with Vlad Dracula.

Another link between the historical and fictional Draculas regards impalement. We have discussed the preferred use of this by Vlad Dracula as a torture method, but for the fictional Dracula, it is he who should be the victim. There is not, however, any possible way of suggesting that the impalement by means of a stake through the heart for a vampire is derived from Vlad Dracula's use of this, given all that has been discussed in previous chapters on the evidence, from Saxon and Viking periods for example, of driving a stake into a suspected undead being.

Even Dracula's death and subsequent burial is shrouded in myth. It is generally assumed in works on Vlad Dracula that he is buried at the monastery on the island at Snagov, near Bucharest. It is often written that Dracula frequently visited Snagov, donated money to it and used it as a safe haven when fleeing his enemies. It was thought that archaeological excavations in 1933 by Dinu Rosetti had discovered the grave of the Impaler, situated inside the monastery at Snagov, just in front of the present altar. Upon lifting the large stone slab, however, Rosetti discovered the grave to be empty, save for a few animal bones. Either Dracula had risen from his grave in true vampire style, or his body had been moved; or it was never there at all, and therefore this was not Dracula's grave. Nevertheless, a burning candle and portrait of Dracula are continually on display next to this tomb, and the legend that this is Dracula's final resting place is still entertained by many.

During the excavations a second grave was discovered in the doorway to the monastery revealing the body of a male, with grave goods that included the fragmentary remains of a purple funerary veil and yellow-brown velvet coat adorned with silver buttons. Fixed to one of the button holes was a golden ring, and a golden thread also attached three small faience buttons decorated with petals of garnet.[33] It was later suggested that this site could be the real grave of Dracula and that the adornments of the skeleton were similar to contemporary examples. Rezachevici summarizes that there was 'no inscription, no indication that the anonymous grave belonged to Vlad Ţepeş. Rosetti, the archaeologist, left not even the slightest reference for such an identification. His excavations of June–October 1933 revealed nothing on Vlad'.[34] It is most likely that although the grave may be contemporaneous with Dracula, it is not that of Dracula himself.

Further to these findings, the research revealed the existence of an earlier church at Snagov, dated to the rule of Voivode

Vladislav I, between 1364–76, since a coin of this period was discovered under the southern foundations of the second church.[35] The first church was repaired by Mircea the Great and documentary evidence also reveals that donations were made to the church by Mircea as well by Dan II, cousin of Vlad Dracul, between 1428 and 1429, by Vlad Dracul in 1441 and by Radu cel Frumos (the Handsome, third son of Dracul and brother to Țepeș) in 1464.[36] This first church was demolished in 1512 by Basarab and the present monastery erected. There are, though, no documentary links between Snagov and Dracula himself.

Where, if not at Snagov, was Dracula buried? To suggest a reasonable hypothesis it is first necessary to understand the nature of the events surrounding Dracula's death. The Romanian historian Nicolae Iorga argued that his death took place near Balteni in the Ilfov county, just north of Bucharest, and many of the later investigations took this as gospel. It is becoming increasingly possible that in this theory Iorga was mistaken, and that it was Vlad Dracul, the father, that was killed at Balteni. However, it may be that this Balteni was not the place near Bucharest, but rather the village of the same name much further north in Dambovita county, perhaps half way between Bucharest and Dracula's princely court at Targoviste, for documentary evidence suggests that Iancu of Hunedoara travelled south from Targoviste in the winter of 1447 and caught up with and killed Vlad Dracul *before* he reached Bucharest.[37] This fits nicely with the geography and is further supported when considering the details of Vlad Dracula's final battle, which suggest that on seeing his forces overcoming the Turks, he climbed a nearby hill to watch the proceedings and was cut off from his army, and later was killed either by his own men, who mistook him for a Turk (highly unlikely, one has to agree), or by an assassin or traitor. Given that the landscape surrounding the Balteni region just north of Bucharest is relatively flat and void of hills, it is more likely that the battle took place south of

Bucharest at another village named Balteni (of which there is only one south of Bucharest), especially since the opposing army had been marching north from the Danube. Rezachivici's theory is that Dracula was buried at another of the monasteries that he founded, Comana in the Vlasca county, based on the notion that his killer, Basarab Laiota (the leader of the Romanian army aiding the Turks against Dracula), would hardly send his body away to a distant monastery that he had no actual links with when one of the churches he himself founded and donated to was in the vicinity. It is certainly a fair theory, and one that has much more likelihood than those others based on myths or legends, even if they are more easily marketed. Unfortunately, the church at Comana has long since been destroyed, but excavations in the 1970s revealed much of the layout and structure, and the remains of a tomb. To his credit, Rezachevici resists the temptation to suggest that this is Dracula's tomb, merely commenting that it *could* be, or if not, that the tomb has yet to be discovered, or was possibly destroyed along with the church in the sixteenth century.

Despite the synonymity in the West of the name Dracula with vampires, there is no evidence to connect them. Because the Western view has been affected by historical propaganda and Hollywood kitsch, it is unable to see the real man. The Romanian take on the subject is the total opposite: they simply know Dracula for what he was, a patriot and hero, and are therefore unable to see the vampire. It is necessary to travel back in time exactly one hundred and ten years, to 1897, to find the truth:

In the same century when the true image of Vlad Ţepeş
– a harsh but just Prince, valiant defender of his country's
independence – was restored to history by a Romanian
historiography in the service of national emancipation and
formation of the unitary national state, another character

Statue of Vlad
Dracula, Târgovişte,
Romania.

was born in Western Europe – altogether different from
the former, an imaginary character named Dracula due to
an unconspicuous English writer.[38]

Perhaps this is the difference; the East see Vlad Dracula as
a good man and the vampire as evil, whereas the West see both
as evil, and unless that changes, the 'Dracula as vampire' myth
will remain. Perhaps this Western view was a direct result of the
Enlightenment reforms that created such hostility towards sub-
jects such as torture and witchcraft from the eighteenth century
onwards, and Stoker's revival of the historical Dracula helped
fuel the ruler's barbaric image in the West. Stoicescu's view is

that the two Draculas are completely different characters with no relationship to each other, and the many works on the subject attempting to go 'In search of Dracula' seem futile. If Stoker had not renamed his Count Vampyre at the last moment, there would be no 'Dracula' to search for. In the words of Gabriel Ronay, 'Vlad the Impaler must, therefore, be exonerated of vampirism and restored to the rank of European monarchs who, although cruel and savage to a degree, have gone down in history as benefactors of their nation.'[39] Only then can he rest in peace.

# SIX

# From Myth to Reality: The Vampire of Folklore

The forest he had heard was a place of dread, for the other villeins
had told terrible tales. Of monsters who flew by night and hid in
dark thickets by day to snap up unwary travelers . . . these evil things
might take any shape. Thousands of villages believed in such wicked
sprites . . . that sooty old crow flapping over the furrows, or the
raven who came and sat on a clod and cocked his beady eye at Jack
as he was ploughing, might be a witch or a wizard come to see if
he could do some evil trick — not a wild bird looking for the worms
which the plough turned up.

Henry Gilbert, *Robin Hood*

If Vlad Dracula was not the source of the modern form of
vampirism, we must look elsewhere for evidence of how the vampire was transformed from the medieval revenant into the form
we recognize so well today in Western society. This evidence is
no more apparent than in the reports on vampiric activity from
Eastern Europe. Throughout much of the later seventeenth
and eighteenth centuries there were reports of vampire epidemics in Eastern Europe, the first in Istria in 1672, followed by
Prussia (1710, 1721, 1750), Hungary (1725–30), Silistria (1755),
Wallachia (1756) and ending in Russia in 1772.[1] Travellers and
returning soldiers brought back these tales and superstitions to
fascinated audiences, spreading westwards into Italy, Germany,
Spain, France and England. The countries where the epidemics
were most prominent had just become integrated into the
European empire from the 'disintegrating Ottoman Empire',
and this may go some way to explaining the spread of these
tales of horror and death.[2] Although there are undoubtedly
differences between each country's reports, for instance, in the

ways in which vampires are created, there are marked similarities in their traits, particularly the folkloric elements. One such widespread example is the description of the vampire being swollen and bloated, as if gorged on fresh blood. Another common theme amongst folkloric vampires is the recurring visitations to family members by the recently deceased 'vampire', who usually pesters them and brings malevolence, ill luck or death.

The scale and longevity of these reports caused a considerable amount of interest among the great thinkers of the period. On 1 November 1765 the *Gazette des Gazettes* put forward a challenge to the scientific community to 'provide conclusive evidence'[3] against vampires and settle the argument for good. Given the emerging scientific abilities of the period, this should have been a straightforward task, and yet in carrying it out scientists were somewhat hampered by society's refusal to abandon superstition and mysticism. This was a period when secret and ritualistic mystical societies, such as Freemasons, thrived in Western Europe, and this acceptance of superstition perhaps aided society's love affair with the mystery of vampirism. Yet the general view in the West was one of disdain, and many were horrified that academic and learned professionals were getting involved in such a ridiculous debate; obviously vampires did not exist. The view from the East, however, was quite the opposite. Nicolae Paduraru suggests that his colleagues and his fellow Romanian researchers were 'baffled by Western attempts to explain the vampire in a rational, Cartesian and materialistic' manner.[4]

It would be apparent, then, that there is still somewhat of an East / West divide on the subject. It is easy to see both sides of the argument; the traits of 'vampirism' can certainly be linked with natural examples of decomposition, of disease or plague, or other scientific methodology as put forward by the West, and yet it appears too coincidental that in every case of

19th-century folklore staking.

reported 'vampirism' the exhumed body had conveniently remained in a non or slow-decomposing state. This could have been the case in, for example, recently buried corpses, but some reports suggest some bodies to have been exhumed after a year.[5] (Of course, it could also be argued that many more bodies were disinterred but were found to be decomposing naturally and so were not documented as they could not be vampires.)

Barber puts forward the idea that logic and rationalism can be falsely applied to mask the actual cause of the events one is trying to explain. For example, if one exhumes a dead body that is bloated and has blood around the mouth then one 'logical' interpretation is that the person has consumed lots of blood.[6] Another example, and one that can be confirmed by the discussion earlier that the vampire can adopt other forms, is that if some malevolent deed occurs and it is deemed the work of a vampire, and yet no vampire is present, then the vampire is an invisible vampire, or if a cat is present then the vampire *is* the cat. This appears incredible, but corroborates everything that is witnessed in reports and beliefs of folklore, and suggests that the possibilities of a vampire's involvement in any given situation is limitless. When one understands this factor it is much clearer to see how the vampire, through folklore and superstition, was able to become such a widespread and feared being.

One must also consider the idea that the body does not simply stop functioning once death has occurred, but continues to move, change and function for some time during the decomposition process until all that remains is the skeletal assemblage. This is, in essence, a return to the primitive ideas attributable to the prehistoric period (see chapter Two), ideas that are alien to us today, given our separation from death within society. These ideas did not entirely disappear with the end of the prehistoric era, but rather moved 'underground', so to speak, and are evident in the early foundations of the scientific evolution. In *Murder after Death: Literature and Anatomy in Early Modern Europe*, Richard Sugg discusses the practice of 'corpse medicine', which was particularly prevalent in the seventeenth and eighteenth centuries, and was adopted by well respected philosophers, scientists and physicians such as John Banister

(Queen Elizabeth's surgeon) and the chemist Robert Boyle. Corpse medicine involved the use of human remains, *mummia*, and human blood to combat diseases such as epilepsy, and throws up an interesting parallel with vampirism, not just in the consumption of blood, but the source of this blood. This source was most beneficial if it was 'the cadaver of a reddish man . . . whole, fresh without blemish, of around 24 years of age . . . dead of a violent death',[7] which Sugg attributes to the notion that the deceased would have died in a healthy state and so would be untarnished by disease or age. This reflects the idea of the ancient demons choosing the pure blood of children to prolong their own lives, and may have some bearing on the idea of vampires being created through a violent death, such as Caligula.

One interesting point of note is that concerning the vampire's mouth, or more precisely the teeth, and the consumption of blood. A great deal of the characteristics relating to the vampire epidemics have been linked to the symptoms of plague and disease, most notably the symptom of having blood around the mouth. Barber explains thus: 'the pneumonic form of the plague causes the victim to expel blood from the mouth . . . the observer does not realise that the blood comes from the lungs but instead sees it as evidence that the body has been sucking blood from the living'.[8] The more traditional view from those who dismiss the scientific explanations still expresses the belief that the vampire has been drinking blood; 'the lips . . . will be markedly full and red . . . [and the teeth] gleam long, sharp as razors, and ivory white. Often the gaping mouth is stained and foul with great slab gouts of blood . . . the offal of last night's feast'.[9]

Not only is this an evident contradiction of the explanation put forward by Barber, but the idea of the vampire's huge teeth is also a fallacy. In folklore it is rare to find examples of the 'long, sharp teeth' common to the literary vampire, and indeed, it may be fair to suggest that in reports from the vampire epidemics we find that certain areas are exaggerated or falsified. For instance, people at the time could have assumed that sharp teeth would have been a necessity for vampires to be able to bite in order to drink the blood, but this could well have been merely an assumption that vampires drank blood in this manner; in Russian folklore the vampire had a sharp, pointed tongue which lacerated the victim in order to obtain blood.

The vampire of folklore must have held its roots somewhere, and science can go a long way to explain the traits of vampirism. There is an interesting theory that it was the victims of the disease porphyria in the Middle Ages that were the foundation of the vampire phenomenon. Symptoms of the disease include photosensitivity (an aversion to sunlight), paleness of the skin, hairiness and elongated teeth, all themselves attributes associated with vampires. It is suggested that the victims consumed blood in order to combat the disease as it introduced haem elements into their systems (haem is a pigment in oxygen-carrying red blood cells).[10] This is yet another example of the consumption of blood for its healing properties and reiterates exactly why the drinking of blood is deemed so important for the vampire in his quest for everlasting life. It is therefore curious to note that the hunt for blood is not an ever-present factor within fables and tales from folklore.

In *Ion Creanga*, a journal of Romanian folklore, we hear in the story of 'The Girl and the Vampire'[11] how the vampire was initially a man who was forbidden to marry his love by their families and so hanged himself from a tree, thus becoming a vampire. His sweetheart, though she loved him, was too frightened to have a relationship with an evil spirit so sought a way to end his nightly visitations (these visits were not in the hunt for blood as one might expect, but merely to be with the woman he loved and to engage in sexual acts with her). The story is full of the characteristics of folklore, the visits to family members, rising from the grave and the bringing of death but has none of the more 'iconic symbolism' of vampirism, such as the fanged teeth and the drinking of blood.

Again, in the Russian folk tale 'The Coffin Lid',[12] we see a different motive to the vampire's visits. In this tale the vampire boasts to the *moujik* (Russian peasant) that he has been into the village and killed a couple of youngsters, but not for the privilege of consuming their blood; indeed, we get the notion that he has done it merely as an act of viciousness and cruelty. He tells the *moujik* that in order to revive the youngsters he must cut off the left skirt of his shroud, pour some live coals into a pot with the piece of shroud and set it alight. The smoke from this will then revive the children. This is interesting as again there is no suggestion that the vampire craved his victims' blood, but there is an idea that the victims themselves could actually be revived from a vampire attack. This lends to the notion that if a purposed 'victim' of a vampire was actually the victim of some disease, they could make a full recovery from this, even if the remedy in the tale is worked in for effect, through the aid of rest and medicine.

One of the first documented cases of a vampire to be reported in the West was that from Joseph Pitton de Tournefort's[13] *Relations d'un Voyage du Levant (A Voyage into the Levant)* of 1717. In this Tournefort gives his first-hand account of a curious ceremony he witnessed on the island of Mykonos: 'We were present at a very different scene, and one very barbarous, which happen'd upon occasion of one of those "vroucolacas"[14] Corpses, which they fancy come to life again after their Internment'.[15]

Tournefort's narrative of an autopsy of a vampire suggests the perpetrator's lack of medical knowledge, with the town butcher (described as a 'clumsy fellow') making his incision in the belly instead of the breast and then searching the entrails, looking for the corpse's heart. During the autopsy, Tournefort describes how it was necessary to burn incense in order to mask the abominable stench, and mentions how the butcher remarked on the warmth of the deceased.[16] Both of these points are interesting to note from a medical point of view, as they can be linked to standard ideas on decomposition, and it was Tournefort's belief that the entrails remained warm as they were indeed rotting, hence the awful smell. The islanders, however, took these details as signs that the corpse was not entirely dead.

The autopsy concludes with the heart being burned, which should (according to folklore) end the vampiric visitations. Curiously, however, it did not. Instances of purposed vampiric activity continued, resulting in many townsfolk leaving their homes, until Tournefort and his companions suggested a close watch should be kept at night to discover the cause of the altercations, and sure enough 'they caught a few Vagabonds, who undoubtedly had a hand in these disorders',[17] leading one to wonder whether the suggestion of a resident *vroucolacas* was exploited by looters and petty thieves. The plague eventually ended when a visiting *Albaneze* helpfully suggested that the practice of placing swords over the grave of the *vroucolacas* (apparently yet another way of rooting out the vampire, which they did three or four times a day) was useless as they were using 'Christian swords' (where the blade, hilt and quillon (cross-piece) form the shape of the Christian cross) and that this was preventing the Devil leaving the corpse.

The body of the suspected *vroucolacas* was eventually burnt on a great pyre of wood covered with pitch and tar. Tournefort comments: 'what they had left of this miserable carcass was thrown into this fire, and consumed presently; 'twas on the first of January 1701. We saw the flame as we return'd from Delos: it might justly be call'd a Bonfire of Joy, since after this no more Complaints were heard against the vroucolacas'.[18]

Perhaps the most famous of the early vampire reports, however, are those of Arnold Paole (sometimes Paul) and Peter

Plogojowitz, the former report being the earliest example of the word 'vampire' in the English language (1732). One possible reason for the documentary evidence of the epidemics being of such influence to European society is due to parts of Serbia and Wallachia being integrated into Austrian possession. The soldiers stationed there to retain possession of these areas became aware of the strange local custom of exhuming dead bodies and 'killing' them. Reports were then made on these by the literate, which in turn created a more widespread interest on the subject.

The report on Paole, entitled *Visum et Repertum* ('Seen and Discovered'), was compiled by Johann Flückinger, an Austrian army surgeon, and details how after serving in the army in Greece and the Levant, Paole returned to his native village of Medvegia in Serbia in 1727. Suspicions arose as Paole harboured little interest in the prospect of marriage to a neighbour's daughter, Mina, but eventually succumbed to pressure. The report then suggests that Paole confessed to his new bride that he had been visited by a vampire whilst stationed in Greece, and that although he had destroyed it and taken preventative measures, such as eating dirt from the vampire's grave, he felt he was cursed from then on. A few weeks later, Paole was dead of a broken neck, the victim of a fall from a haywagon.

Within a month there were numerous sightings of Paole in the village and four deaths were attributed to him, which caused such unrest that officers from Belgrade were summoned to exhume the corpse. The following account is based on Flückinger's report:

> The body had moved to one side in its grave, its jaws were open, and blood was trickling from its mouth. The officers and the church sexton sprinkled garlic on the remains and drove a stake through its heart, whereupon a dreadful scream issued from the body and blood gushed forth.[19]

Gypsy village on the River Arges.

While these actions ended Paole's visitations, it was stated that Paole had attacked some cattle also, which people had then eaten. Over the next three months, seventeen people died from this. Interestingly, it is the mention of the blood around the mouth that may lead us to think that Paole had signs of the plague, as put forward in Barber's theories, and could well explain why so many people died over a short period. The majority of our information on the case of Paole comes from Flückinger's report, but additional information is present in a letter from Johann Friedrich Glaser to the editors of the German magazine *Commercium Litterarium*, dated 13 February 1732. Glaser informs the editors that his son, a doctor from Vienna, was sent to investigate the case of Paole in December, 1731 one month before the official Flückinger Commission. In the letter, Glaser senior describes how 'completely normally-buried dead people rise from their graves and kill . . . these in turn rise and kill also . . . this happens in the following way: the dead attack the sleeping at night and exhaust them of blood, so that all die on the third day'.[20] This mention of a three-day illness matches information provided by Flückinger and is perhaps indicative of a specific disease.

Glaser also informs his editors that his son was able to perform an autopsy on one of the bodies and found that the entrails were healthy and intact, and that the stomach and lungs were full of blood. Details of the seventeen people who died, taken from Flückinger's report, reflect similar symptoms to that of Glaser's, such as the body of a 20-year-old woman named Stana, a 60-year-old woman named Miliza, a 17-year-old boy named Joachim and a mother and 18-day-old baby to name but a few, all of whom had the same symptoms: blood in the stomach and chest (lungs). There is, however, a discrepancy among the bodies and that is from Flückinger's body number thirteen, Stanoika, a 20-year-old who again died after a three-day illness. What is strange about this body is that during those three days Stanoika claimed she had been visited by one of the other deceased, who had throttled her (this is a common theme in later vampire literature). On inspecting the body, Flückinger noticed a blood-shot blue mark, approximately the length of a finger, on the right side of the neck directly under the ear. Two other bodies, numbers nine and ten, were both found to be fully decomposed; yet nothing is made of this point in Flückinger's report, which simply states that they were returned to their graves after the investigation. The details of the report, and indeed the case in general, all point to the villagers being the victims to some form of disease or plague, and that the deaths were mistakenly attributed to a case of vampirism due to a lack of medical knowledge and an overtly superstitious people. Once the autopsies were completed, the heads of the bodies were cut off by local gypsies and burned along with the corpses, after which the ashes were scattered into the river Morava. Six years later, another vampire epidemic broke out, resulting in more exhumations; here too, the heads were cut off and the bodies burned.

The report on Peter Plogojowitz from Kisolava in Serbia (1725) is similar to that of Paole. Shortly after his death, Plogojowitz is deemed to have returned and visited certain villagers, all who died within twenty-four hours. Once again the body is exhumed, found to be in a preserved state and 'the hair and beard – even the nails, of which the old ones had fallen away – had grown on him; the old skin, which was somewhat whitish, had peeled away, and a new fresh one had emerged under it. The face, hands, and feet, and the whole body were so constituted, that they could not have been more complete in his lifetime.'[21] The body is staked through the heart, causing blood to gush from the ears, nose and the wound. This is identical to the condition that Arnold Paole was found in when he was disinterred.

It is stated in Imperial Provisor Frombold's report on Plogojowitz that after his death he visited his wife and asked for his *opanki* (shoes), and again this is similar to other examples from folklore, where the reasons for the vampire's visits were for anything but the drinking of blood. However, Frombold states that when the body was dug up there was fresh blood around the mouth, which according to common observation he had sucked from those killed by him. There is also a strange passage in Frombold's report whereby he states that after Plogojowitz was staked not only did blood gush forth but there were 'other wild signs' *(wilde zeichen)* which he 'passed by out of high respect' in his report, and in this he was most likely referring to the corpse having an erection. This is the only example of note in the vampire reports of a sexual element, a theme that again becomes more prevalent within the vampire literature of the nineteenth century.

There are many elements of folkloric vampires that can certainly be explained by scientific doctrines, and we have seen in the cases of Arnold Paole and Peter Plogojowitz that reports of blood around the mouth and in the lungs are most likely indicative of a form of pneumonic plague. There are, however, some

19th-century folklore staking.

areas that are confusing, such as the documented levels of decomposition. It has been noted that many of the examples of suspected vampires have been in a non- or slow-decomposing condition, and this has often been related to soil conditions. In the case of Arnold Paole, two of the bodies had decomposed naturally, as was expected, and these were re-interred and claims of vampirism dismissed. Yet all the bodies examined by Flückinger would have been buried in close proximity given that they were all from the same small village. It also appears miraculous that time and again the suspected vampire corpses had all (with noted exceptions) remained in a largely intact condition, and this is far too convenient to be entirely conclusive.

Perhaps the most telling factor, though, is the similarity between not only the characteristics of folkloric vampires, be that returning from the dead to visit family and friends, the state of the corpse after exhumation or the methods required to end the plague, but similarities between actual cases or examples of vampirism across varying countries, evident in Russia, Romania, Serbia and Greece. That there can be such clear parallels between the examples, when it would be nigh on impossible for communication between the isolated rural villages, is indicative that the phenomenon of vampire belief has undiscovered causes. For if vampirism can be entirely explained by current scientific or medical doctrines, how is it that certain common elements are apparent in examples from these countries that cannot be explained by, for example, plague? How is it that the dead are time and again witnessed in their villages after their deaths, or how is it that victims complain of being suffocated or crushed by a presence? This last point may be explained by a fever perhaps, but the evidence noted by Flückinger of the finger-sized bruise on one victim's throat suggests more than this. There is certainly more to the phenomenon of the vampire of folklore, which the West too easily dismisses as a matter of peasant naivety.

What can be noted from the three cases discussed is the common concern of breaching laws, rules or general religious practice relating to the dead bodies deemed to be vampires, particularly in defiling them by removing the heads or staking the body. The similarities between Tournefort's account and the report on Plogojowitz in relation to the level of mass hysteria created by the vampire reports reflect just how far the worry of vampirism affected society (albeit a particular area of society). It is most likely that both Paole and Plogojowitz were victims of some plague or disease, but the reports are highly useful for they allow us an insight into the beliefs and fears of people in relation to the vampire of folklore, the being that undoubtedly led to the creation of one of the most revered monsters of literature.

That vampirism took hold of people's fascinations throughout Europe is without a doubt, and yet it was hoped that the great debates on the subject would put an end to the matter. Although the emerging sciences of the period hoped to prove conclusively that there were no such things as vampires, rather a series of medical conditions that were not understood by largely primitive peoples, society had to have remained moderately superstitious and fascinated by the unknown, else the new Gothic literature would not have been received so well. The response to the challenge of proving or disproving the existence of vampirism involved some of the great philosophers of the age, such as Voltaire and Calmet, and it was the treatises by such men that perhaps brought the interest in the subject to an end. The reason was that rather than promote the idea of vampirism, which the early eighteenth-century reports were doing, they attempted to explain and debunk the phenomenon. Some even went as far as to ridicule the whole situation, quite poignantly evident in Voltaire's take on the matter:

> What! Vampires in our Eighteenth Century? Yes . . . In Poland, Hungary, Silesia, Moravia, Austria and Lorraine . . . there was no talk of vampires in London, or even Paris. [The] true bloodsuckers did not live in cemeteries, they preferred great places . . . Kings are not, properly speaking, vampires. The true vampires are the churchmen who eat at the expense of both the king and the people.[22]

Perhaps the most important of the treatises was Calmet's, as he was a well-respected religious scholar and theologian, but yet again the response to this was divided. The reason that Calmet's opinions on the matter upset so many of his contemporaries was just that he was so well-respected; his critics could not believe that someone so prestigious was getting involved in the pointless debate of vampires. Many of these critics had the notion that the best way of ending such a frivolous concept was to ignore it. Calmet's conclusion was, quite admirably, that he could not deny the idea of vampires given all the evidence, but that there was no solid proof either. It may appear that he was just 'sitting on the fence' so to speak, but in actuality he was only admitting what most are not brave enough to do, and that is that although vampires are most likely not 'real', the idea has been around for so long and affected so many that there is still that small element of uncertainty as to their actual existence, and it is this uncertainty that is almost certainly the life-force of the vampire, real or not.

Around 1770 the debate had pretty much run its course and the idea of vampirism within society eventually died down. The exact reason for this remains uncertain but it may be related to the conflict and political turmoil of the following few decades. This was after a fifty-year period of interest and discussion, a considerable period in itself, given that the vampire was seen by many as an unbelievably irrelevant and preposterous notion. These critics would be proved wrong, however, as it took the vampire a mere forty years to be reborn within society once again in the form of the literary vampire, a guise which has proved to be its strongest yet.

# A Fiend is Born: The Vampire in Literature

*The strength of the vampire is that people will not believe in him.*
Abraham Van Helsing, *Dracula*

During the nineteenth century the vampire was immortalized within literature as he was made the subject of poems, magazines and novels. The sheer scale of the interest fuelled by earlier debates on the question of vampirism led to an extensive list of vampiric literary work.[1] This noted, there are perhaps only four examples that remain influential and important texts on the development of the vampire literary genre, and indeed in turn influenced later stage and film adaptations. These four texts, then, are John Polidori's *The Vampyre*, James Malcolm Rymer's *Varney, the Vampyre*, Sheridan Le Fanu's *Carmilla* and Bram Stoker's *Dracula*.

It can be seen that the earlier poetry of the Romantic movement was the foundation for the vampire in literature, work by authors such as Shelley, Keats and Southey. Whilst examples of vampires in the Age of Enlightenment had been based heavily on scientific methodology and deductive reasoning, the foundations of horror in the Romantic period encouraged the use of imagination and feeling and were highly influential for the Gothic genre. Indeed, Polidori's *The Vampyre* was influenced by an earlier poem of Lord Byron's entitled 'The Giaour', in which we hear:

> But first on earth, as Vampyre sent,
> Thy corse shall from its tomb be rent,
> Then ghastly haunt thy native place,
> And suck the blood of all thy race.

which was most likely influenced itself by earlier Romantic works such as Samuel Taylor Coleridge's 'Christabel' or 'The Rime of the Ancient Mariner'. These works by Coleridge contain interesting ideas on a prolonged 'life in death' and cursed eternal wanderings that are remarkably similar to those found in vampirism, and it is therefore easy to see how it may have influenced later vampiric literature.

Polidori's tale was in essence the first 'vampire story', drawing on elements that were present in folklore, to which were added other ideas, such as the vampire being an aristocratic member of society, that would become central to all later vampire stories. The American historian David J. Skal describes *The Vampyre* as being 'one of the most imitated and influential horror stories ever published',[2] whereas Christopher Frayling goes further and believes it to be 'probably *the* most influential horror story of all time'[3] and 'the first story successfully to fuse the disparate elements of vampirism into a coherent literary genre'.[4]

So, briefly, let us understand the plot before examining its influence on later vampire stories.[5] At the many London parties being held a Lord Ruthven appears,[6] a 'nobleman more remarkable for his singularities, than his rank',[7] who becomes the interest of society:

> his peculiarities caused him to be invited to every house
> . . . [particularly] his face, which never gained a wanner
> tint, either from the blush of modesty or from the strong
> emotion of passion.[8]

The subject of the story, Aubrey, also comes to London at that time, a man who had 'that high romantic feeling of honour and candour'.[9] Aubrey and Ruthven meet, become friends and set off to travel together. At first Ruthven appears generous, 'his companion was profuse in his liberality',[10] and kind, but Aubrey's guardians (his parents were killed earlier in his life) send letters begging him to leave Ruthven. These confirm his suspicions that all is not right with Ruthven and he leaves, halting Ruthven's marriage to an Italian lady in the process.

Aubrey then travels to Greece, where he meets a girl by the name of Ianthe, with whom he falls in love and hopes to marry. When he is caught in a storm at night, he takes shelter in a woodland hut, where he hears 'the dreadful shrieks of a woman mingling with the stifled, exultant mockery of a laugh'.[11] This turns out to be a vampire who has attacked Ianthe, the girl he heard, who had followed Aubrey to protect him from the vampire, but who dies due to the attack. Aubrey finds at the scene 'a naked dagger of a particular construction'.[12] Due to the loss of Ianthe, Aubrey is bedridden with a violent fever. Lord Ruthven then appears at Athens and, hearing of Aubrey's illness, tends to him until he recovers. They then travel again but are attacked by robbers and Lord Ruthven is mortally wounded, but before he dies, he makes Aubrey swear an oath not to reveal his secrets for a year and one day, to which Aubrey agrees: 'Swear by all your soul reveres, by all your nature fears, swear that for a year and one day you will not impart your knowledge of my crimes or death to any living being in any way, whatever may happen or whatever you may see'.[13]

Ruthven is laid on a stone under the moon, a curious wish, but when Aubrey learns of this and goes to the stone Ruthven is gone. Aubrey is bewildered but cannot explain it, so travels home alone, taking with him Ruthven's personal effects. Among these is a case of weapons that includes a sheath for a dagger 'ornamented in the same style as the dagger discovered in the fatal hut'.[14] Once home and reunited with his loving sister, Aubrey attends a function where, with horror, he encounters Lord Ruthven, the same man he had left for dead in Greece. At this, Aubrey is distracted and his oath plays on his mind continually, so much so that he becomes 'neglected, and wandered as often exposed to the noon-day sun as to the midnight damps'.[15]

Aubrey is bedridden through mental illness as he learns of Ruthven's proposal of marriage to his sister, but due to his oath is unable to warn her or their guardians. Finally, through despair, Aubrey is left 'emaciated, his eyes had attained a glassy lustre'.[16]

Aubrey makes one final attempt to save his sister, bribing his servant to take her a letter, but the servant instead gives it to his physician, who thinks it the product of mad ravings. He then manages to give his guards the slip on the morning of the wedding, but encounters Lord Ruthven on the stairs, who promptly hurries him back to his room, whispering 'remember your oath, and know, if not my bride to day, your sister is dishonoured. Women are frail!'[17] The rage that courses through Aubrey due to his helplessness breaks a blood-vessel, and his life slips away before him, but not before he has summoned his guardians and related his story. The guardians rush to save Miss Aubrey, 'but when they arrived, it was too late. Lord Ruthven had disappeared, and Aubrey's sister had glutted the thirst of a vampyre!'[18]

It could well be that in Lord Ruthven Polidori created the prototype vampire.[19] All later creations seem to follow this 'Ruthven formula'. Nevertheless, 'Polidori's style, an unusual combination (for the time) of clinical realism and weird events, was also influential, and (like the author) has been much neglected'.[20] This appears a contradiction, but may be due to the controversy surrounding *The Vampyre* at the time of its release. Written in 1816 it was not published until 1819 in the *New Monthly Magazine*, under Byron's name. The two had a strained relationship (Polidori had been Byron's physician), and Byron immediately disassociated himself from the story.

This was eventually cleared up as the work later released as the story *Fragment* and penned by Byron shows similarities to *The Vampyre* but was merely a ghost story told at the infamous gathering of Byron, Shelley, Polidori, Mary and Claire Claremont at Byron's villa on the shore of Lake Geneva, where Mary

Shelley (then Godwin) wrote what would later become *Frankenstein*. Although the two stories follow a similar pattern, it was Polidori who developed the myth, yet it is *The Vampyre* that appears the more simplistic of the two. For example, regarding the oath, in *The Vampyre* it lasts 'a year and a day' but in *Fragment* it is more complex, involving a ring the vampire wears and the ninth day of the month. Perhaps this is why Polidori was able to create a better story, as he discarded the chains of complexity and in using a simpler plot was able to appeal to a wider audience. F. W. Murnau's 1922 vampire film, *Nosferatu*, is one of the most powerful film adaptations based on this early formula, and yet is markedly simpler than many of the later creations that are not seen as iconic, hinting to why Polidori's creation proved so influential.

It could be suggested that *The Vampyre* was written during Polidori and Byron's 'serious personal disagreement',[21] and may therefore indicate that Ruthven (if indeed he was based on Byron) appeared much worse than he may have done. The result is a villain who is suave and aristocratic yet dangerous and alluring, the so-called 'Ruthven formula' that is apparent in many vampires from that point. The story may also be the first time that the vampire's victims have solely been women; the folkloric vampires did not differentiate between sex, or age for that matter, as we have seen.

One of the most noticeable points in *The Vampyre* is that the vampire is the victor and all the pure and strong 'innocents' die, something that is reversed in later literature such as in *Dracula*. Also, unlike later offerings, there is little in the way of folkloric elements and almost no use of 'classic' vampire associations such as the graveyard or castle. There are, however, certain elements that can be noted in *The Vampyre* and in *Dracula*, namely the similarities between Aubrey and Jonathan Harker, both of whom are quite easily intrigued but soon become suspicious and fearful; and Lord Ruthven and Count Dracula, who are

Gary Oldman as Count Dracula in *Bram Stoker's Dracula*.

both mysterious and darkly fascinating. There are also parallels between Ianthe and Mina Harker, both of whom the vampire attempts to steal away, Dracula for love, Ruthven for destruction and perhaps revenge.

*The Vampyre*'s success is perhaps due to the fact that it in many ways rekindled the interest in vampires[22] and thus paved the way for later 'classics' such as *Carmilla* and *Dracula*, both of which are more well-known than Polidori's offering, but without which they would not have existed in the forms they are in. It also paved the way for the vampire on the stage in 1823.[23] The final word on *The Vampyre* shall be left to Polidori himself, who died at the age of 26 in 1821 after reportedly drinking prussic acid after an illness suffered due to a head injury.

Mr Editor,

As the person referred to in the Letter from Geneva, prefixed to the Tale of the Vampyre, in your last number, I beg leave to state, that your correspondent has been mistaken in attributing that tale, *in its present form*, to Lord Byron. The fact is, that though the *groundwork* is certainly Lord Byron's, its development is mine, produced at the request of a lady, who denied the possibility of any thing being drawn from the materials which Lord Byron had said he intended to have employed in the formation of his Ghost story.

I am, &c, JOHN W. POLIDORI[24]

If the vampire witnessed in Polidori's tale bears little resemblance to its folkloric predecessor, then the arrival in 1847 of *Varney, the Vampire*[25] certainly made amends. For, whereas *The Vampyre* insinuated horror, *Varney* created it. The difficulty faced by author James Malcolm Rymer, bearing in mind that *Varney* was nigh on 850 pages long and spanned 237 chapters, was how to keep the reader interested. Released as a series of 'Penny Dreadfuls', Rymer took the 'Ruthven formula' created by Polidori, but made some notable additions (a method also adopted by Stoker for *Dracula*).[26] Many of these changes utilize folkloric elements such as the appearance of the vampire, which is a 'figure tall and gaunt' with a 'long, gaunt hand which seems utterly destitute of flesh',[27] drawing parallels with the 'undead' of folklore. This is similar to the openings of *Dracula* and also to the vampire in *Nosferatu* (which is based on *Dracula*).

In the opening scene of chapter One between the vampire and the girl, there appears to be an underlying sexual theme, as well as the obvious 'shock horror', something which is prominent in later 'vampiric' works (and most obvious in *Carmilla*, as shall be discussed later): 'the smooth skin of that fair creature, just budding into womanhood, and in that transition state which presents to us all the charms of the girl'.[28] This is suggestive of an almost pure, virginal quality. This is furthered once the vampire has gained entry into her room, showing him to be of 'gigantic height', while the girl 'places one small foot on the floor',[29] contrasting their sizes and depicting the vampire as dominant. The entire scene reflects a sexual tension that builds into a climax when the vampire bites the girl in an episode that is suggestive of rape. This is an idea that continually appears in vampire literature and films, leading some to suggest that the biting of the throat by the vampire is a metaphor for sexual intercourse, an act deemed too risqué actually to be depicted in the nineteenth century; 'with a plunge he seizes her neck in his fang-like teeth – a gush of blood, and a hideous sucking noise follows. The girl has swooned, and the vampyre is at his hideous repast!'[30]

It would seem that Rymer therefore took the theme of sexuality hinted at by Polidori, with Aubrey and Ianthe perhaps or Ruthven and his conquests, and moved it on further; whereas Ianthe was merely killed, in *Varney* Clara (the girl of the story) is turned into a vampire, and this conjured further horrors within the literary vampire. Another addition used by Rymer (or rather a change to the trends evident in most other literary works) is that rather than the 'heroes' of the story hunting the vampire, it is the 'angry mob', an alteration that may reflect examples from folklore, particularly regarding the idea of 'noble vampires' living in castles or large houses that are segregated from wider society, and who become the object of suspicion from the locals (the angry mob) who are later utilized in film: 'The vampyre, the vampyre, death to the vampyre – death and destruction to the vampyre',[31] chanting which no doubt echoes that heard in the witch hunts of the Middle Ages.

Later in this chapter we have another description of the new female vampire: 'look at the bloom upon her lips, why her cheeks are fresher and rosier than ever they were while she was alive.'[32] This is markedly different to the 'tall, gaunt figure' witnessed earlier and this contrast is often apparent in vampire literature. Indeed, it perhaps indicates two stages of vampirism, the first, just described, the initial period where the vampire is in its prime, newly converted to vampirism and striving towards immortality. As the realization of what this means dawns on the vampire, as is apparent in *Varney*, it starts to despair and crave friendship or love. This leads to a second stage, where the vampire is in need of revivication, either through this love or through the quenching of its thirst for blood. These stages do not always come in this order, however; in *Dracula* the Count first appears in the aged and gaunt guise and later is revitalized.

And so, once it is realized that the vampire is trapped to torment the living forever, the mob realize it must be destroyed, and this is to be done in true folkloric style: 'a vampyre is quite as secure buried in a cross-road with a stake through its body'.[33] We do, however, hear that it is difficult to believe that the vampire, Clara, is just that, as the only tell-tale sign is 'the blood upon the lips, and the very fresh-like appearance of the face'; this has parallels with the vampire epidemics of the eighteenth century and could be explained by the scientific theories put forward earlier. This appears again when the vampire is staked: 'the eyes of the corpse opened wide – the hands were clenched and a shrill, piercing shriek came from the lips'.[34]

*Varney* is perhaps the only literary work on vampires that really attempts to make the reader empathize with the vampire's desolation and despair until the pioneering *Vampire Chronicles* by Anne Rice one hundred and fifty years later. Towards the end of *Varney* and after the destruction of the vampiric Clara, Varney himself confesses to Mr Bevan, the priest, his remorse in his acts and his vampirism, speaking first about Clara herself:

And has it come to this? Is this my work? Oh horror! Horror unspeakable. In this some hideous dream or a reality of tragedy, so far transcending all I looked for, that if I had tears I should shed them now, but I have none . . . I thought that I had steeled my heart against all gentle impulses . . . but it is not so.[35]

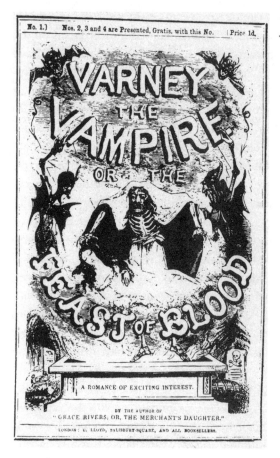

Cover of James Malcolm Rymer's *Varney, the Vampire*.

Finally, he tells Mr Bevan that 'More than once have I endeavoured to cast off this horrible existence' and 'what should I pray but for the death [that] has flitted from me in mockery?'.[36]

In the end the despair becomes too much for Varney, who hires a guide to lead him up to the summit of Mount Vesuvius where he finishes his vampiric plight once and for all 'Before the guide could utter anything but a shriek, Varney took one tremendous leap, and disappeared into the burning mouth of the mountain'.[37] Not only was this the end of Varney, it was also the end of the early literary vampire type, as 'all the various plays, poems, stories and operas which exploited the commercial potential of Polidori's Vampyre (by authors such as Charles Nodier, James Planche, James Malcolm Rymer, Alexandre Dumas and Dion Boucicault) simply reworked the Ruthven plot'.[38] Although certainly a winning formula, and still utilized in later works, it was perhaps becoming a little stale in a demanding genre, thus necessitating a new twist. This was provided by J. Sheridan Le Fanu in *Carmilla* in 1872.

*Carmilla*, 'the most famous and certainly the most influential among vampire tales . . . second only to Bram Stoker's *Dracula*',[39] is the earliest example of a vampire story to reflect signs of lesbianism. It is perhaps fitting as a precursor to *Dracula* as it combines the sexual undertones of *Varney* with the more traditional horror types: such as the undead sleeping in its coffin and the biting of the victim. *Carmilla* is also perhaps the first vampire tale where one feels a sort of empathy with the vampire; although this is true, to a certain degree, of *Varney*, nevertheless his foul deeds distract the reader from this. As Carmilla herself is portrayed as a young and innocent girl whom we do not know to be a vampire for quite some time, it is easier to understand her feelings and emotions, especially her need for friendship and love.

In the story, the main character describes how when she was a child of six years old she had a strange nightmare in which she was visited by a young lady in her bed who caressed her through her discomfort and soothed her to sleep. She awoke to the sensation of two sharp pricks upon her breast and cried out in alarm. The young lady quickly withdrew onto the floor and, presumably, under the bed. When the girl's attendants rushed into the room and heard her tale, the girl 'could perceive that their faces were pale with an unwonted look of anxiety' and saw them 'look under the bed and about the room'.[40] Clearly they understood that the situation implied a vampiric visitation.

Illustration from *Carmilla* by D. H. Friston in the magazine *Dark Blue* (1872).

With the arrival of Carmilla at the girl's home some years later as a result of a rather curious incident involving a coach accident, the girl is shocked to discover that Carmilla and the young lady from her dream are one and the same. Although they soon strike up a friendship, it is clear that much deeper emotions run between the two:

> Dearest, your little heart is wounded; think me not cruel because I obey the irresistible law of my strength and weakness; if your dear heart is wounded, my wild heart bleeds with yours. In the rapture of my enormous humiliation I live in your warm, and you shall die – die, sweetly die – into mine.[41]

These are the words spoken by Carmilla, reflecting her intentions towards the girl, of which we have no doubts when she follows these with 'you are mine, you shall be mine, you and I are one for ever'.[42]

Although this hinted homosexual longing is a new direction within vampire literature, there are also clear reflections of atypical traits, folklore for example, highlighted in the peasant-girl funeral procession on which we hear 'she is the poor girl who fancied she saw a ghost a fortnight ago, and has been dying ever since, till yesterday, when she expired'.[43] It is interesting that the peasant girl was said to have been visited by 'a ghost' rather than a vampire, but this is evident for much of *Carmilla*, perhaps heightening the suspense by not revealing too much until the end. It is again strange when the two girls are offered charms which they both 'instantly purchase'; 'will your ladyships be pleased to buy an amulet against the oupire, which is going like the wolf, I hear, through these woods?'.[44] The fact that Carmilla buys one, a vampire herself, is rather surprising and mirrors much later portrayals of vampires in the twentieth-century, who are depicted as immune to the cross, for example.

There are notable similarities between *Carmilla* and *The Vampyre* in the oath that Carmilla is sworn to by her mother – 'I am under vows, no nun half so awfully, and I dare not tell my story yet, even to you'[45] – and also with the incident in chapter Six, where the girl sees a shape moving around her bedroom at night, and two 'broad eyes' appear before her face, followed by a sharp pain in her breast, after which she lays there 'more dead than alive' (this also has parallels with Elizabeth Wojdyla in the Highgate Case, see chapter Ten). It appears that *Carmilla* is again influenced by earlier offerings and in turn influences later examples, and this is the case for the majority of vampire novels. It is interesting that whichever one considers, be it *The Vampyre*, *Varney*, *Carmilla* or *Dracula*, it will be described as being *the* most influential or *the* most imitated vampire story, and one cannot help but believe it to be true of each in turn upon reflection.

An obvious later influence from *Carmilla* can be seen in the use of the anagram 'Millarca' or 'Mircalla' and the parallels in the Hammer Horror film *Dracula 1972* where the main character is

'Johnny Alucard', itself an anagram of Dracula. Remaining with the theme of Countess Mircalla, there are again similarities with the historical Dracula, Vlad Tepes, as both had their heads cut off and both of their bodies were found to be missing from their reopened graves. Although there are debates on the extent to which Vlad Dracula was used as an influence for Bram Stoker's novel there are, so far as I am aware, no suggestions of a link between Vlad Dracula and *Carmilla*.

In chapter Fifteen of *Carmilla* we hear from the General: 'You have heard, no doubt, of the appalling superstition that prevails in Upper and Lower Styria, in Moravia, Silesia, in Turkish Servia, in Poland, even in Russia; the superstition, so we must call it, of the vampire'. This is perhaps the most obvious example that Le Fanu did indeed use the folkloric beliefs and that, like its predecessors, it was using earlier fears and public interest as a promotional tool. Perhaps the one factor that sets *Carmilla* apart is the use of lesbianism, but each of the four vampire works discussed utilized some unique angle that sets it apart from the others, and this is the most likely reason that all four are as influential in the horror genre as each other. And so, we must finally consider what is certainly *the* most famous of all vampire novels, if not *the* most influential, Bram Stoker's *Dracula*, and the town of Whitby, North Yorkshire, which was integral to Stoker's masterpiece.

# EIGHT

# Vampiric Haunts #2: Whitby, North Yorkshire, England

The town of Whitby is described by its residents as being made infamous worldwide by the fact that Bram Stoker set part of his classic novel *Dracula* there. People across the world visit Whitby as they come in search of Dracula: some even believe Stoker's evil Count to be buried there (interesting, as in the novel Count Dracula is killed in Transylvania and explodes into dust, making it impossible for him to be buried anywhere).

Whitby has, to an extent, welcomed this notoriety with guided vampire tours and the 'Dracula Experience' on 9 Marine Parade, two popular vampire-themed activities. There is also the 'Whitby Dracula Society', a group dedicated to the macabre who hold twice-annual Gothic Weekends and the 'Dance Macabre', a Gothic Ball.

## THE TOWN OF WHITBY

The town had long had a history of the supernatural before Stoker brought Dracula there; indeed, it is suggested that the area is one of the most haunted places in England. There have been numerous ghost sightings in Whitby, perhaps the most famous being that of Constance de Beverley, who is said to haunt Whitby Abbey. The legend goes that she was walled up in the Abbey's dungeon and left to die, the price paid for an illicit dalliance with a young knight.[1] The shrouded ghostly figure of

Whitby Abbey.

St Hilda, the founder of the Abbey who died in AD 680, has also been sighted in one of the windows. It is interesting, then, that Stoker did not use the Abbey in *Dracula*, though some of the characters do mention it; Mina Harker, in her journal, for example. On visiting Whitby, however, it becomes somewhat clearer why as the Church of St Mary, the church used in *Dracula*, is certainly more ominous and imposing, perched precariously on the edge of East Cliff, its graveyard crammed with large tombstones and grave markers. It is here that Mina sights her friend Lucy seated on their favourite bench in the middle of the night during one of Lucy's sleepwalking episodes: 'There was undoubtedly something, long and black, bending over the half-reclining white figure'.[2] This is the Count, who is drinking away Lucy's life-force, and is symbolic of the age-old adage of black and white, of dark and light, of good and evil. Fitting, then, that this should take place on consecrated ground; Stoker is suggesting that Dracula is truly a mighty evil.

St Mary's church, Whitby.

The 'Dracula Trail', composed in co-operation with Mr Bernard Davies of the London Dracula Society, allows visitors to Whitby to experience the sights and settings of Stoker's novel: the Abbey and St Mary's Church, the 199 steps leading to the two, the Crescent where Lucy and Mina were staying (which is where Stoker stayed during his holiday there in 1890), the fishmarket and the bridge. It also guides people to the two vantage points integral to *Dracula*: the Bram Stoker Memorial Seat at the southern end of West Cliff, situated in the area where Stoker sat and viewed Whitby when getting ideas for his novel, and the bench in St Mary's graveyard directly opposite Stoker's Seat on East Cliff, an excellent place not only to view the town of Whitby but also to sit and read *Dracula*.

Abraham Stoker was born in Clontarf in Dublin Bay in 1847, at 15 The Crescent (the street had the same name as the one he stayed in at Whitby and used in *Dracula*). Until the age of eight he was more or less bedridden, the victim of a mystery illness, when he made an unexplained recovery and grew into a six foot two healthy young man who excelled at sport. After completing an honours degree in Science, he followed his father, Abraham Stoker senior, as a clerk at Dublin Castle. Whilst studying for a Masters degree and becoming leader of the Philosophical and Historical Societies at the University, Stoker took an interest in the theatre, where he saw Lord Henry Irving perform and, being rather aghast at the lack of reviews, complained to the *Dublin Mail*. His reward was to become the theatre critic for the *Mail* (unpaid and uncredited, however) and later for other journals. When Irving returned to the Dublin Royal some five years later Stoker's review led to a long and lasting friendship between the two and a job managing Irving's Lyceum Theatre in London.

The Lyceum Theatre took Stoker to the pinnacle of London society and it was from this position that he was able to become a part-time author. However, although propelled into the spotlight so to speak, Stoker was forever in Irving's shadow, but was 'oddly content' with this position.[3] On a personal level, friends of Stoker described him as being a loyal friend and a scrupuously fair businessman; a jovial giant with a flaming red beard that contrasted the darker hair of his head.[4] There are suggestions that Stoker modelled his famous Count on Irving, who was widely reported to be debonair and masterful, with the uncanny ability of feeding off other people's energy. The debate on this will perhaps go on for some time, but as many of the ideas for *Dracula* were based on real-life events, experiences and people, this suggestion is highly plausible.

Stoker got many ideas for *Dracula* whilst holidaying in Whitby in 1890 but his research incorporated much more than this holiday alone. In 1890 Stoker also met a professor from Budapest University, one Armeniur Vanbery, who, it is reported, discussed at length with Stoker ideas on vampirism and the occult as well as regaling him with tales of his travels in Eastern Europe and particularly Transylvania, and of the history of Romania and Vlad Tepes, the Impaler. There is a wide debate as to what extent Vanbery influenced Stoker's settings and characters for *Dracula*; Stoker could well have used Vanbery's descriptions of the area and possibly of Bran, but there are no direct links between Bran Castle, Vlad Țepeș and *Dracula*. There is also a suggestion that Stoker may not have heard of

Vlad Dracula from Vanbery at all, but rather found the name in a book he borrowed from the library at Whitby.

Yet others believe that Stoker relied heavily on Vanbery's offerings; 'he seems to have given Stoker the idea for Dracula and provided him with much information which Stoker supplemented with reading from the British Museum'.[5] Stoker himself appeared 'not dark or evil' but rather a 'pleasant, affable and unassuming chap, the complete opposite of his famous protégé'.[6] His other works include *The Snake's Pass* (1890) and *The Jewel of Seven Stars* (1903), but were it not for *Dracula* (1897) it is quite probable none of his offerings would be remembered today.

### DRACULA

Feelings on *Dracula* as a literary work remain divided; it is widely accepted as a classic text and yet it certainly has its share of critics. Montague Summers summed up the scepticism on the book when he commented that 'It is well-nigh impossible for a story which deals with the supernatural or the horrible to be sustained to any great length . . . the first part, "Jonathan Harker's Journal", is most admirably done, and could the whole story have been sustained at so high a level we should have had a complete masterpiece but that was scarcely possible'.[7] This does seem a touch unfair, but undoubtedly these first four chapters are in essence the jewel of the work and once captivated by them it is difficult not to see the whole novel through. There is a section after the events in Whitby when Stoker does seem to lose his way a little but this is more than regained later in the book when Van Helsing is on the trail of Dracula. It could be further suggested that it is the subject matter rather than the literary aspects of the book that draw and redraw the reader into the story, and this is supported by the reception to *Dracula* on the stage; the first production was considered poor and yet it proved successful.

Many believe that *Dracula* did more to resurrect the vampire at a time when interest was waning than any other book and, as I stated earlier, it is this ability to re-invent itself that has given the vampire its longevity. Indeed, this perhaps ironic 'immortality' re-created by *Dracula* has in many ways transformed the vampire into an icon, something which it would be extremely difficult to now forget in modern society.

When *Dracula* was re-issued in 1983 as a classic text, A. N. Wilson wrote somewhat apologetically in his introduction to the work, 'Dracula, is, patently . . . not a great work of literature. The writing is of a powerful, workaday sensationalist kind. No one in their right mind would think of Stoker as a "great writer". How can someone who is not a great writer be said to have written a classic? [By making] your hair stand on end. And that, from the first page to the last, is what Dracula is meant to do'.[8]

Perhaps one of the keys to *Dracula*'s long-term success, for it was by no means an instant hit, was its ability to blend the old with the new. It can therefore be viewed as the crossover between historical vampirism and modern vampirism. Although the idea of the vampire as we know it today had been gradually building within literature for some years, it was not until the release of *Dracula* and its subsequent adaptation for the theatre and cinema respectively that we witness any great widespread association between the vampire and the imagery created by the aforementioned Ruthven formula. The way ancient traditions, such as the folkloric elements of vampires or the influence of the early demon forms (evident in the similarities between the three vampire women at Castle Dracula and the ancient vampires such as Lilith or the Lamia) were intertwined with cutting edge technology, such as the use of shorthand, Dr Seward's phonograph and Van Helsing's blood transfusions, allowed for the creation of what was in essence the vampire's passport into the twentieth century and its manifestation once again as a socially relevant being. This was really quite remarkable, as many assumed that vampire literature had run its course and people were generally becoming bored with the genre, a factor that is supported in the number of 'tongue in cheek' vampire satires released in the run up to the publication of *Dracula*, such as Paul Féval's *La Ville-Vampire* (1875), rather like *Buffy The Vampire Slayer* in the twenty-first century.

There are, certainly, if read closely enough, clear social meanings within *Dracula*. Consider the characters: the stalwart and somewhat tactless professor, the young and wholesome solicitor, the selfless doctor, the good wife who has learnt how to make a living, all who unite to combat the oppressor. For the last hundred years, Britain had been doing just that in her struggles against the French and this would continue against the Germans in the upcoming Great War. The vampiric theme has often been utilised in this way, with Turgenev and Tolstoy compiling folkloric vampire tales depicting the Cossacks and landlords as vampires in Tsarist Russia, for example.[9] The underlying theme of *Dracula* could well be that of another Christian imperialistic crusade; 'whether the Satanic Lord was dominating and self-destructive or supine and self-destructive, the literary (as opposed to the folkloric) vampire he represented may well have had something to do with attitudes towards (and projections from) English imperialism'.[10] Could this be one of the reasons for *Dracula's* success?

The social implications of a work such as Stoker's *Dracula* fit nicely into a wider European context; Karl Marx rather gratuitously used the vampiric icon in his *Das Kapital*, with phrases such as 'Capital is dead labour that, vampire-like, only lives by sucking labour and lives the more, the more labour it sucks'. Maybe, therefore, it is fitting that Marx was to be buried at Highgate Cemetery, London, where Lucy Westenra was laid to rest after being transformed into a vampire by Count Dracula (and which was also the home of the infamous Highgate Vampire as we shall see later in the final chapter of this work).

Later in *Das Kapital* Marx attempted to further his point by comparing the lord–peasant relationship in the Danubian principalities with that of the 'Wallachian Boyar', who was, rather unsurprisingly, none other than Vlad Dracula himself.[11] With the English translation of *Das Kapital* first released in 1897, the timing worked out rather well for *Dracula*'s release in the same year.

As has been mentioned there is little evidence to suggest that anything more than Vlad Dracula's name was used by Stoker, and yet there are a few curiosities, if perhaps incidental. Given the history of Vlad Dracula, it is interesting when, in 'Jonathan Harker's Journal', Stoker writes 'in his speakings of things and people and battles, he spoke as if he had been present at them'.[12] This could be viewed as some evidence to suggest that Count Dracula was indeed Vlad Dracula, although the Count later states he is a 'Szekelys' whereas Vlad was not. The Count also comments that 'Attila's blood courses his veins' and Vlad Dracula was a noted admirer of some of Attila the Hun's methods, so there are certainly some links – though these are a little tentative.

The most likely explanation, though, is that Stoker utilised many areas of his research and combined the best bits into a sort of vampiric hybrid. There is no reason why the Count could not be a culmination of certain characteristic traits from Henry Irving, with certain historical attributes from Vlad Dracula. Rather than being based on Vlad Dracula, Stoker could merely have selected salient points from Romanian folkloric customs, garlic and rosary beads for example, as in the incident from chapter One with the blue lights. This is based on what Stoker read in Emily de Lazowska Gerard's 'Transylvanian Superstitions' (1885) where she describes a Romanian tale whereby 'in the night preceding Easter Sunday witches and demons are abroad, and hidden treasures are said to betray their site by a glowing flame',[13] a notion also depicted in a conversation between Count Dracula and Jonathan Harker. A final point

Original cover for Stoker's *Dracula*.

worth considering is that up until Stoker had nearly finished writing *Dracula* the count was merely called 'Count Vampyre' and the first chapters were set in Austria rather than Transylvania.

No matter whom the characters are based on or where Stoker's ideas came from, the story of *Dracula* remains. Love it or loathe it, it is certainly one of the most famous stories ever written, be it a classic text or otherwise, and is perhaps the only occasion where all the different aspects of the vampire, from

Max Schreck as
Count Orlok in
*Nosferatu*.

history, folklore and literature, combine. Having stressed this point, however, it was not until the mass-market technology of cinema, which allowed for the widespread success of the *Dracula* films starring Bela Lugosi and Christopher Lee from the 1930s onwards, that any really widely accepted vampire form became apparent. Indeed, earlier vampire films such as Murnau's *Nosferatu* (1922) ignored the Ruthven Formula iconography entirely. Had it not been for Stoker's novel the vampire we all recognize today may never have existed.

Count Dracula is without doubt the most famous vampire ever created and regardless of what came before or after him, this is probably how the vampire will be remembered forever. Mention the word 'vampire' and the image created by Count Dracula always springs to mind. It is, for most, not important that Polidori created this vampiric guise or that Le Fanu heavily influenced Stoker, or indeed that the vampire has some six thousand years of history prior to *Dracula*, and it is this that emphasizes just how important Stoker's work really is.

# NINE

# Phantasmagoria:
# The Modern Vampire

Look abroad – the moon shines bright,
We and the dead ride fast by night
Gottfried August Burger, *Lenore*

Today the vampire is no longer the feared being that he once was. In the hundred years or so post-*Dracula* the vampire's transformation has been like a star turning into a supernova; after the gradual evolution of the vampiric being over thousands of years this final chapter in the evolution has progressed rapidly. The fear created by the vampire has dissipated, and the vampire himself has become a parody of what he once was. The reason for this is quite simple: we no longer fear the vampire. It was society's fear of the vampire that allowed him to exist through the ages. But how did the fear subside after so long? And what does this mean for the vampire in the twenty-first century?

Although *Dracula* was the catalyst for the modern vampire myth it was almost uniquely the theatre, cinema and television exploitation of the being that ultimately caused the shift towards the modern conception of the vampire. Whereas in the superstitions and myths of the Middle Ages or within folklore it was the lack of knowledge that fuelled the existence of the vampire, the technological advancement and mass-market productions of modernity eradicated the unknown and transformed the vampire into a household product. The vampire is used to promote everything from breakfast cereals (Count Chockula) to children's television (Mona the Vampire), to tourism, and is the subject of endless books, films and television programmes. In fact, such is the current widespread appeal of the vampire that the majority of people today have not only heard of the vampire, but could also describe how he looks. And ninety-nine times out of a hundred you can bet that the description will include a cape, fangs, bats and a thirst for blood. Why is it, then, that this imagery has been adopted out of all the ones discussed? And how many people, although instantly recognizing Count Dracula, have actually read the book or are at least familiar with the story? The answer to these questions must be sought in the vampire's progression within cinema, a development that undoubtedly ended our fear, but that also created an entirely new vampire in the twenty-first century.

*Dracula* was a gruesome literary product that reflected late Victorian England; London had witnessed one of the most sadistic serial killings in its history through the infamous 'Jack the Ripper' murders. Although it is suggested that the incident was a media hoax, the report from the Central News Agency of a woman being attacked by a 'well dressed man' who seized her by the throat again throws up parallels with Stoker's creation.[1] At the time some even went as far as to suggest that

> it is so impossible to account . . . for these revolting acts of blood that the mind turns as it were instinctively to some theory of occult force, and the myths of the Dark Ages rise before the imagination. Ghouls, vampires, bloodsuckers, and all the ghastly array of fables which have been accumulated throughout the course of centuries take form, and seize hold of the excited fancy.[2]

The result of *Dracula* was a renewed scholarly and public interest in the vampire. Important works on the subject, such as Dudley Wright's *The Book of Vampires* (1924) and Montague Summers's *The Vampire: His Kith and Kin* (1928) and *The Vampire in Europe* (1929), sought to document the vampire's history in various cultures and provided first-hand examples of the superstition.

It was also during the 1920s that *Dracula* was adapted for the big screen, albeit somewhat illegally, in the Expressionist German filmmaker F. W. Murnau's *Nosferatu: eine Symphonie des Grauens* ('a symphony of horror') in 1922 starring Max Schreck: 'Nosferatu! Doesn't this name sound like the very midnight call of Death? Speak it not aloud, or life's pictures will turn to pale shadows, and nightmares will rise up to feed on your blood', explains the opening caption. Although the film is considered an adaptation from Stoker's novel, the producers did not obtain copyright permission and although the names of the characters and places have been altered it clearly follows *Dracula*'s plot. As a result, the courts ordered all copies of *Nosferatu* to be destroyed, although several had already been distributed, allowing the film to not only survive but also to become a vampire classic and collectors' item.

There are, however, some quite striking alterations in *Nosferatu* from the original story, most notably the appearance of the vampire Count Orlok. The first time he appears in vampire form he is extremely sinister, has a huge form that fills the doorway and his features are quite rat-like, with protruding teeth, pointed ears and long, pointed fingers; here the vampire is more akin to the undead of folklore than the vampire of literature, in many ways mirroring the image evident in *Varney*. It is really the only example where the traditional vampire was preferred to the 'Ruthven formula' version, and may be one of the factors why the film proved so popular. Count Orlok is portrayed in the same way as Varney (lonely, desperate and condemned), and the viewer is encouraged to empathize with him – an idea later utilized by Anne Rice in her *Vampire Chronicles*. *Nosferatu* also added its own iconography that remain associations within vampire films: the dark and foreboding shadows, the prolonged movements of the vampire, the 'reaction shots' that occur when a moment of horror occurs.

Although more like the folkloric vampire in appearance, Orlok does have some 'classic' modern traits such as waking at night, sleeping in a coffin and biting his victim's neck. With regards the plot, it does follow that of *Dracula* in general with Hutter (Harker) travelling to Transylvania, Land of the Phantoms, to finalize the sale of some property to Count Orlok (Dracula), but in Wisborg, Germany rather than London. Hutter's employer, Knock (who takes the place of both Harker's employer Hawkins and Dracula's minion, Renfield) suggests that he knows Orlok is a Nosferatu when he tells Hutter that by travelling to Transylvania he could make money, although it may cost him a 'bit of pain and a little blood'.

And so Orlok buys the house, attacks Hutter and travels to Wisborg onboard the *Demeter*, where he kills the crew. At this point Van Helsing makes a brief appearance giving a lecture on the 'vampire plant', the Venus Fly Trap, but this is all we see of him. Missing too are the characters of Dr Seward, Lord Godalming, Quincey Morris and Lucy Westenra and Mina Harker becomes Ellen Hutter. Another difference is the use of rats and the arrival of the plague alongside the vampire, a clear link with folkloric examples; rats themselves are known to have introduced the bubonic plague or Black Death in the fourteenth century. The ending of *Nosferatu* is also markedly different from *Dracula* in that Ellen (Mina) discovers she must entice the vampire into sunlight to destroy him and so sacrifices herself to do this. Orlok is distracted whilst drinking Ellen's blood and misses the cockcrow, thus exploding into dust with the break of dawn, ending the plague. This is similar to the popular myth that not only is sunlight lethal to vampires, but that the plague and death brought about by them can only be stopped by destroying the vampire.

Two years later, in 1924, a theatre version of *Dracula* was released in the form of Hamilton Deane and John Balderston's *Dracula: The Vampire Play* and, although an extremely spare version of *Dracula* (set in only two locations: Dr Seward's parlour and Carfax Abbey), the play was a great success and was instrumental in persuading Universal Studios to create *Dracula* on the big screen. It was this version, written by Tod Browning and released in 1931, and starring the Hungarian actor Bela Lugosi as Count Dracula, that transformed the image of the vampire forever. With the stage version, Deane realized that the opera cloak would not only have a great dramatic effect but could be used to cover hidden trap-doors as Dracula disappeared under the stage. Lugosi decided to carry the prop over into the screen version and the cape has now become as iconic for the vampire as fanged teeth or the stake that pierces the heart.

It is worth noting, however, that Lugosi was not Browning's first choice, with popular actor Lon Chaney the preferred candidate. Sadly Chaney succumbed to throat cancer in 1930 and Lugosi, the star of the Deane / Balderston stage show, eventually persuaded his way into the role (perhaps due to him agreeing a considerably lower salary than might be expected). The production was also hit with a reduced budget due to studio finance difficulties, which in effect meant not only were a number of scenes cut from the final film, but that there was less money for salaries, a factor that may have determined Lugosi's inclusion. One of the most memorable and widely recognized features of the film is Lugosi's rolling East European speech pattern; 'I am Drrra-cul-aaa', which many attribute to the fact that he did not speak English and therefore had learned his lines phonetically. Lugosi's portrayal of Dracula is a chilling performance; his accent, facial expressions, threatening yet sophisticated demeanour and grandiose attire are still widely associated with vampires today. The horror he brought to the role was such that on the opening night many members of the audience fainted, a factor that undoubtedly had the producers sweating. They need not have worried, for *Dracula* proved an instant success and paved the way for further horror films by Universal including *Frankenstein* (1931), *The Mummy* (1932) and *Dracula's Daughter* (1936), the sequel to *Dracula*. Perhaps it is fitting that when Lugosi died in 1956 he was buried in one of his Dracula capes.

Bela Lugosi as Count Dracula, from the 1931 *Dracula*.

Jorg Waltje suggests that '[Lugosi's] portrayal of Dracula as a foreign predator in the guise of aristocratic sophistication became the role model for many vampires to come [within the cinema]',[3] but although this may appear the case, this 'role model' had already been created in the 'Ruthven formula' within literature, and only the vampire image created by Murnau disrupted this trend, albeit rather briefly. This image was further enhanced by the number of Dracula-related films made by the British Hammer Horror corporation from 1958–74,[4] starring Christopher Lee and Peter Cushing. The films were often praised for their visual style, although were rarely taken seriously: 'Altogether this is a horrific film and sometimes a crude film, but by no means an unimpressive piece of melodramatic storytelling' wrote one critic of *Dracula* in *The Times*.[5]

Much like the initial reaction to its literary counterpart, however, many critics of *Dracula* found it disgusting and vulgar, which is strange given the success and popularity of the novel and the stage adaptation, and the consequent cinematic versions of *Nosferatu* and Universal's *Dracula*. The media deemed it a 'singularly repulsive piece of nonsense' that was made in 'such sickening bad taste',[6] and the *Daily Telegraph* sarcastically commented that a new certificate rating be created for it; 's' for sadistic or 'D' for disgusting.

The making of *Dracula* was not without its restrictions; the censoring board demanded that there should be no scenes depicting the vampires' sinking their teeth into the victim's neck and that the act of staking the vampire should be depicted out of shot. Also, they demanded that women should be properly clad and there be no scenes of a sexual nature. Sex was

Advertising poster for Terence Fisher's 1958 *Dracula*.

something they believed there was no room for in a horror film. After watching a preliminary black and white rough cut of the film, the Board made further requests to remove the scenes showing the staking of Lucy, Dracula's seduction of Mina and the closing destruction scene of Dracula.

Hammer's response was to remind them that the x certificate suggested for *Dracula* would automatically prevent anyone under the age of sixteen from seeing the film and to argue that the audience expected a certain amount of horror and gore from the film. They also suggested that the proposed cuts would remove the excitement and shocks that the audience were expecting. Hammer's *Dracula* therefore relied heavily on the sexual side of vampirism for the first time and was the first film to show a vampire baring its teeth.

Changes from the novel and previous efforts included Jonathan Harker being portrayed as Van Helsing's assistant and posing as a librarian at Dracula's ancestral home. Key scenes, such as Dracula's journey on the *Demeter* to Whitby, were left out. It is mentioned in Hammer's *Dracula* that vampires cannot change themselves into bats, wolves or other such creatures, a notion that is used heavily in other productions and is contrary to popular opinion. This is contradicted in Hammer's next vampire film, *Brides of Dracula*, however.

Hammer's *Dracula* is generally considered a worthy effort, given its budget, and, with the full use of the Technicolor process and star performances by Christopher Lee and Peter Cushing, it remains one of the classic vampire horror films in cinema. The success was not to last, though, and eventually Lee became somewhat disillusioned by the direction in which the films were going. He quit after *The Satanic Rites of Dracula* (1973), after which only one more 'Dracula' film was released by Hammer. Once again the vampire genre in general was becoming stale and audiences began to lose interest, but the vampire resurrected itself and was thrown back into the spotlight in the form of

Christopher Lee as Dracula, from *Dracula A.D. 1972*.

Anne Rice's novel *Interview with the Vampire* (1976), the first part of her now best-selling *Vampire Chronicles*. In this we hear the story of the vampires Louis and Lestat and how they become a 'vampire family' when they turn Claudia, a young girl who loses her mother to the plague, into a child-vampire. The story is markedly different from any other vampire narrative that came before it and is a deeply dark, disturbing and soul-searching masterpiece that is second only to *Dracula* in dragging the vampire into the modern world. What it created was a personality for the vampire, a kind of desperate being that was continually struggling to understand its cursed existence; a theme that was only once hinted at before in *Varney*.

The 1970s revival also saw a remake of *Nosferatu* by the German filmmaker Werner Herzog entitled *Nosferatu: Ein Phantom der Nacht* (*Nosferatu: The Vampyre* in English) starring Klaus

Kinski as Count Orlok. The film was a fitting tribute to the original and made its own mark on the Dracula theme. As the copyright on Stoker's novel had by then expired, Herzog was able to use the original character names, but he stayed true to Murnau's film in most other respects. Notable additions saw modern vampire imagery exploited, perhaps due to a more widespread understanding of vampires (courtesy of the Universal and Hammer offerings no doubt), such as the use of the bat and the cross, and rather than Orlok's (Dracula's) vampire status being surmised for much of the film, his vampire guise is apparent from the start. These common associations are further depicted when Orlok is staked by Van Helsing (he was killed by sunlight in the original), and when it is suggested that Christian symbolism is all-powerful against the vampire: the vampiric Harker is unable to leave the circle of Communion wafers and Orlok shuns the cross after leaving the *Demeter*. The film is not quite sure of its logic on this point, though, as it also shows Orlok entering a church and Harker ripping off the cross he wears around his neck. The main point that can be drawn from the re-make is that although it is in effect a re-release of a world-famous classic and should therefore be guaranteed a degree of success, Herzog still deems it necessary to include common contemporary vampire themes and mythology in order to satisfy his audience, and this suggests that by the 1970s society had a firm idea of what a vampire should be, something that the literary, theatrical and cinematic versions of *Dracula* must be credited with.

Due to this preconceived ideology, future vampire works had to find that extra twist in order to stimulate their audiences. It is likely that everyone who watches a modern vampire film will be familiar with the vampire and perhaps also the vampire film genre as a whole. Writers of modern vampire films use their audience's existing experience and knowledge, but must also strive to provide something different and new, or else interest in the genre would quickly wane. Audiences of the earlier films would have been a lot less familiar not only with the vampire as an icon, but with the cinematic horror genre in general, and this in itself creates an increased capability for inducing fear. And as mentioned, it was Anne Rice's offering that was the catalyst for the next stage in the vampire's journey into the present.

*Interview with the Vampire* without doubt changed the course of the vampire's evolution and, as *Dracula* did with the historical and modern forms, bridged the gap between the early-modern vampire and the present form. After re-inventing itself in the literature of pioneering authors such as Anne Rice and Stephen King, the vampire was born again in the world of the cinema, most notably in Joel Schumacher's *The Lost Boys*, which was released in 1987. It made over US$32 million and won the Saturn Award for Best Horror Film. The film tells the story of a teenager, Michael, who, on moving to Santa Clara with his mother and younger brother, falls in with a gang of vampire punks, oozing attitude and clad in leather and riding motorcycles. From early on in the film there is the suggestion that Star, the only girl of the group, is a form of psychic vampire (discussed in detail shortly) and entrances Michael into falling in love with her. There are yet further examples of psychic vampirism in the mind games played on Michael by the vampire gang leader, who psychologically turns his rice into maggots and his noodles into worms. This is good evidence that the cinematic vampire genre was attempting to develop the common vampire myth, and this is further supported in the creation of vampires through the consumption of vampiric blood in *The Lost Boys*, as opposed to the more traditional view of biting the neck evident in earlier films such as *Nosferatu* and *Dracula*. Once Michael drinks the vampire blood offered to him by the gang, he starts to turn vampire himself. Here we witness many of the common traits associated with vampires such as long fingernails, bad breath, aversion to sunlight and lack of reflection as well as the strange ability of being able to float in mid-air, something that is never really explained to the viewer.

With *The Lost Boys* we see the common theme of darkness, indeed, much of the film is set at night. However, up until the gangs' attack on the beach, vampirism is assumed by the audience rather than shown. There are many vampire associations, such as the garlic, the use of mirrors, the vampire comics and the bat kite, but no actual vampires per se; rather then being explicit, it utilizes the audience's preconceptions. The attack and the gangs' vampiric forms leaves no doubt on the matter, and the scene is full of blood drinking and violence and is accompanied by eerie church organ music to heighten the theme of horror; 'so now you know what we are, you'll never grow old and you'll never die . . . but you must feed!' David, the leader of the gang, informs Michael.

*The Lost Boys* is in many ways a strange vampire film, in that it continually downplays the vampire theme, almost as if it feels it is exploiting its audience's fascination with the subject and is slightly embarrassed by the topic. To compensate for this it adds an element of humour and 'goofiness'. A vampire sneers at the Frog brothers (vampire hunters) that 'garlic don't work, boys!', to which the brothers reply, 'Yeah, well try holy water, death breath!'. A scene involving the vampire child (which could have been deemed bad taste) is made light-hearted with the line 'It's the attack of Eddie Munster!'. These snippets of humour allow the film to be viewed as a satire and, while still a horror film, *The Lost Boys* is a film in which the horror is diluted. This is no more apparent than when the head vampire is being staked and destroyed (a scene deemed too risqué for cinema just thirty years earlier in Hammer's *Dracula*); *The Lost Boys* reduces the repulsiveness of this by showing the Frog brothers donning blacked out swimming goggles to protect them from the splattering blood, thus bringing an element of humour to the scene.

The horror of vampirism is present alongside the 'tongue-in-cheek' humour of it, as has become common in modern dealings with the vampire, despite attempts by *Interview with the Vampire* or *Bram Stoker's Dracula* to maintain the fear element.

The theme music to *The Lost Boys* is the Doors' hit 'When You're Strange' and includes the line 'When you're strange, no-one remembers your name', a phrase that quite poignantly sums up the ailing vampire as the 1980s progressed into the '90s. The success of vampire literature, which introduced us to the 'thinking man's vampire', and films such as *The Lost Boys*, which treated the vampire almost as a figure of ridicule or amusement, could not disguise the fact that the traditional vampire was beginning to lose its relevance in the technological modern world. The answer was, rather unsurprisingly, to resurrect *Dracula* once more.

In 1992 Francis Ford Coppola offered his version of the vampire classic under the title *Bram Stoker's Dracula*. The title itself suggests that the film is a direct adaptation of Stoker's novel and, on the whole, it follows it fairly closely. In fact, of all

Dracula in bat form in Francis Ford Coppola's film *Bram Stoker's Dracula*.

the *Dracula*s, Coppola's is certainly the closest to the original book, but there are notable differences. Many of these are subtle changes: Dracula has a shadow; Dracula and the peasants are depicted as Romanian, rather than Hungarian as in the novel; and there is an addition in the form of Lucy's sleepwalking incident in Whitby, where Mina finds an entranced Lucy and the Count having sex. Whilst these differences were probably added to tie in with modern expectations (the ties between Romania and vampires for example) they do aid further developments in the modern vampire myth. The underlying sexual theme of vampirism that had slowly been building since Victorian literature and that was barely suppressed in the Hammer Horror films was finally unleashed in Coppola's *Dracula*. This led the way for sex to be emphasized much more in future vampire offerings, so much so that it has become rare to find a contemporary vampire film that does not utilize a sexual theme.

One of the most important changes from the novel is the portrayal of Count Dracula as Vlad Dracula and Mina Harker as a resurrection of Vlad Dracula's wife from the fifteenth century. Not only does this promote the false link between the historical and fictional Draculas (and taint Vlad Dracula's reputation in the process), but it offers a specific explanation for Dracula's longing for Mina. Although it is initially Lucy that he targets, attacks and turns vampiric, it is secretly (except to the reader / viewer) Mina that he longs for and his attack on Lucy appears hateful and cruel because of this. In the novel much of this is left to the reader's own speculation, but Coppola's film adaptation attempts to offer us specific answers to some of Stoker's conundrums.

The novel itself ends with Dracula being killed in Transylvania, but here Coppola's *Dracula* continues briefly. One year after Dracula's death, Jonathan and Mina Harker have a child, a baby boy that they name Quincey after Quincey Morris, the vampire hunter, suggesting that the only death amongst the vampire-hunters shall not go forgotten. In Hollywood, good always triumphs over evil in the end.

Though of all the *Dracula* adaptations Coppola's was perhaps the best, it did not win much critical acclaim, gaining Academy Awards for Best Costume Design, Best Make-up and Best Sound Effects Editing, rather than the more respected directing, acting and writing awards, despite an all-star cast which included Gary Oldman, Anthony Hopkins, Keanu Reeves, Winona Ryder and Richard E. Grant. Maybe this was the final death rattle for *Dracula*. It was certainly the last 'traditional' vampire film. Yet there is still that element of closure missing from the *Dracula* journey. Although there have been several adaptations since the novel's release, on both stage and screen, the definitive *Dracula*, a version that remains true to Stoker's original story, is yet to be made. Given the route that the modern vampire has followed in the fifteen years since Coppola's offering, it is uncertain whether it ever will be.

After seventy years of vampire films, it was time for a change. The genre was becoming stale once more and society was losing interest. The arrival, and success, of *Blade* (1998) is a beacon in the darkness of the vampire myth. Gone are the 'old-world' qualities and associated vampire images; there are no grave-yards, no castles, no rising from the dead, no sleeping in coffins. Instead, we are introduced to a gleaming, cutting edge, cyber-

Wesley Snipes as *Blade*.

A female vampire attacks Blade in the Blood Bank nightclub.

vamp who exists on the borders of reality. Blade is still a creature of the night, hidden away from humanity, but his enemies
are no longer stake-wielding professors. Indeed, the standard
apotropaics of garlic, crosses and stakes are no match for the
modern vampire, for whom grenades and machine guns are preferred. Blade (Wesley Snipes) is half-human, half-vampire (a
*dhampir* from legend), the result of a vampire attack on his pregnant mother, and is the ultimate vampire hunter. He is aided in
his quest to destroy all vampires by his mentor Whistler (a kind
of modern Van Helsing-type character), who manufactures the
liquid garlic serum Blade must be injected with to combat his
thirst for blood; while some vampire associations may be mod-
ified in the modern genre, they are not entirely abandoned.

The success of *Blade* was in many ways a precursor for how
vampire cinema morphed into the modern age. It is extremely
rare nowadays to see a film where the age-old vampire traits are
exploited (the Transylvanian Count, the sleeping in a coffin, the
shadowy castle or graveyard), and vampire films now generally
tend to adopt the explosive action-packed thriller formula. All
the successful vampire films that have followed *Blade* have used
this formula: films such as the sequels *Blade II* and *Blade Trinity*;
the *Underworld* films, which pit vampires against werewolves;
and *Nightwatch* and *30 Days of Night*, both of which utilize good

old-fashioned horror. Perhaps the reason for this is that the films are no longer about hidden meanings or metaphorical suggestions, or attempts to psychoanalyse the vampire, but rather about blood, horror and death, a kind of primitive return to the vampire's roots but in a modern sci-fi realm. In essence they are void of deep, complex plots (unlike *Dracula* or *Interview With the Vampire*) and do not require the viewer to carefully analyse the events that unfold, leaving them free to simply enjoy the experience. And maybe this is the key to their success; like the blood-drinking of the vampires they display, watching them is an act of sheer, unadulterated pleasure.

The increased popularity of the vampire, coupled with new mass-communication technology such as the Internet, boosted the growing appeal of the Gothic lifestyle. Before we discuss this emerging sub-culture it is necessary to understand another kind of vampire that was introduced to society – the psychic vampire. It is tempting to label this form of vampire as being 'new' but it is certainly not. The examples discussed in the chapter on Transylvania of vampiric beings that 'fed' on the power or energy of animals or humans have huge parallels with the energy-draining psychic vampire, but only in the psychoanalytical world of the modern vampire does the phenomenon become more easily understood.

Psychic vampires most likely go as far back as the ancient spirit (demon) forms, the Incubus or Succubus, who would drain people of life, energy or blood (similar to Romanian examples of 'power draining' witches). They also visited sleeping people and made them have sinful (that is, sexual) ideas. Often diseases or conditions that lacked visible medical signs – for example, being lethargic, drowsy, melancholic, depressed or generally 'under the weather' – were attributed to these 'psychic vampires'. In the present, doctors would readily link these conditions to causes such as poor diet, tiredness, mineral deficiency, general depression or a more severe cause such as diabetes or leukemia. Yet

opposed to unwilling victims) or commit acts of violence or harm in the name of vampirism.

It is this latter faction, those with the wish to drink blood (sanguinarians) or those that believe they are vampires, that draw society's attention to the darker sides of vampirism, and as these are often a reflection of the widespread vampire myths it becomes difficult for most people to accept that they have a place within modern society. Sanguinarians generally pose no threat within society and are extremely health and safety conscious in relation to obtaining and consuming blood, preferring willing and reputable donors. This is an extremely widespread and complex sub-culture and it is beyond the scope of this work to represent them fairly.[9] The practice of drinking blood by members of modern society should come as no surprise, given all the examples of use and consumption of both animal and human blood throughout history. In the present, though, we tend to view these practices as occultist taboo, given our separation from these pagan practices in everyday life, and so when we do come across them, they are viewed as alien and unwholesome acts. For many, these acts are completely normal, but have to be carried out in privacy in order for their perpetrators to avoid persecution. It is only when these acts come to the surface, such as in occult ceremonies or Satanic rituals or in examples of murder or torture, that society is introduced to them and thus it is difficult for most people to associate any response with these practices other than horror and revulsion, most likely the exact same response to suggestions of witchery or vampirism in the past.

In the West there are numerous accounts of 'vampire crime', that is, cases of murder or sadism that are linked with vampirism, but not all of these warrant the vampire label and it is generally society's misunderstandings regarding the vampire that are to blame. A prime example of this is evident in three such cases from Germany, England and Canada respectively. In 1920s Germany a serial killer terrorized the people of

Düsseldorf on a scale similar to that of Jack the Ripper in London some forty years previously. A number of young girls and women were subjected to sexual assault, stabbings or beatings and many of the stab victims had in excess of thirty stab wounds. The man arrested and convicted of the killings was Peter Kurten, nicknamed by the press 'Vampire of Düsseldorf', and although his first murder was committed in 1913 it was the period between February and November 1929 that was his most active and brutal. Victims of these murders include Rosa Ohliger, an eight-year-old girl, who was stabbed thirteen times and then set alight with petrol; two sisters, aged five and fourteen, who were returning home from a fair when Kurten strangled them, slit the throat of the five year old and decapitated the other; and a servant girl named Gertrude Schulte, who was approached by Kurten and asked for sex, to which she replied that she would rather die. Kurten's chilling response was 'die then', as he promptly stabbed her. Fortunately Schulte survived and was able to give a description of her attacker. In October 1929 Kurten's methods altered somewhat as he raped and beat to death a young woman and followed this up with two hammer attacks a fortnight later. Finally, on 7 November, a five-year-old girl was found strangled and with thirty-five stab wounds. The attacks continued well into 1930, but since Kurten adopted continually changing methods of killing, from strangulation to beatings to stabbings, the police struggled to catch him.

Although undoubtedly a vicious and sadistic serial killer, Kurten showed little if any traditional vampiric traits. His murders were certainly bloody and yet there is no evidence to suggest there was any vampiric link in this; he did not drink the blood, bite his victims nor attempt to obtain their 'life-force'. His motives were apparently purely thrill-seeking; indeed, at the trial, Kurten confessed that he often orgasmed after or upon reflection of the attacks, such as when he set the body of Rosa Ohliger on fire. This begs the question why he was dubbed

'The Vampire of Düsseldorf'. Many of his attacks were committed at night and many involved wounds to the neck, and almost all were exclusively on females (sharing some similarities with the Ripper murders). This must suggest that the press, who made the initial link between Kurten and vampires, must have related his actions to vampires through preconceived ideas on what vampires entail. The preying on young girls or women an~ the ferocity of the attacks are therefore added to the mod image of the vampire and the widespread media attent~ ~n this only helped to tarnish the vampire's image in the ~olic's imagination.

Another example of this misassociation is ~at of John George Haigh, the British killer dubbed t'ie 'Acid Bath Vampire', who dissolved his victims in a bar~el filled with sulphuric acid. Haigh's first victim, a man named William McSwann whom Haigh had previously worked for as a chauffeur, went missing on 6 September 1944. It was later discovered that Haigh had hit him over the head with a hammer and dumped his body in an acid-filled 40-gallon drum, dissolving him into a sludgy liquid. A trail of killings followed, during which Haigh assumed the identity of his deceased victims in order to obtain property and money. This eventually led to Haigh's downfall, when a dry-cleaning receipt for his final victim's fur coat was discovered in his workshop, along with papers relating to his other victims. Haigh was finally hanged on 10 August 1949.

Until his confession, there were no obvious links between Haigh's murders and vampirism. It was not until he realized that, although having no bodies, the police had enough evidence to convict him that he offered the story that suggested a level of vampirism. During this confession, regarding the murder of his final victim Olive Durand-Deacon, he claimed that after shooting her in the back of the head he used a penknife and glass to collect some of her blood, which he then drank.

Haigh confessed to five murders in all, and informed the police that he collected and drank a glass full of blood for each one, claiming that he had an obsession and need for blood and that was why he had killed his victims. He claimed this need for blood stemmed from the head injury he had suffered in a car accident in 1944. This injury bled into his mouth, which Haigh claimed rekindled his childhood fascination with blood, and he began to have strange dreams, similar to those he had had as a teenager. Haigh describes how '[I] saw before me a forest of crucifixes which gradually turned into trees. At first there appeared to be dew, or rain, dripping from the branches, but as I approached, I realized it was blood. Suddenly the whole forest began to writhe and the trees, stark and erect, to ooze blood . . . A man went to each tree, catching the blood',[10] and Haigh goes on to detail how the man approached him to encourage Haigh to drink the blood.

As with the Kurten case, the media was quick to pick up on the vampire connection even though there was little evidence in his crimes that linked him to vampires apart from his own testimony. The headlines of the *Daily Mirror* in 1949 informed us of the 'Hunt for the Vampire',[11] which immediately turned Haigh's case from a simple 'murder for profit' scenario into something much more sinister. Haigh's plan may have been to plead insanity, which his 'vampire' plea would go a long way to help. Unfortunately for Haigh, not only did the psychiatrists that examined him deem him sane, but further evidence suggested that Haigh had researched into the field of insanity and how it could be used to escape a death sentence, perhaps as a back up plan to his *corpus delecti* belief. Haigh also made the mistake of asking one of his interviewing officers 'off the record' whether a person would be likely to be released from Broadmoor, the institution for the criminally insane.

The third case is the only one of the three to show a vampiric theme in the murders themselves, but this again is only loosely based on preconceived ideas. The case relates to a series of rapes and strangulations of young women in Montreal and Calgary in Canada between 1969 and 1971. The man convicted of the crimes was Wayne Clifford Boden, the 'Vampire Rapist'. His first victim was Shirley Audette, found on 3 October 1969 in Montreal; though fully clothed, she had been raped and savagely bitten on her breasts before being strangled. On 24 November 1969 a second woman, Marielle Archambault, was discovered in her Montreal apartment, also the victim of rape and strangulation and with the same horrific bite marks on her breasts. The difference this time, however, was that though she was covered with a blanket, she was naked and had been killed at home, perhaps suggesting that she knew her killer. The previous day her work colleagues had seen her leave work with her boyfriend, known only as Bill, and a photograph of him was found in her apartment. Despite a police sketch of the man being released to the press, the police were unable to discover his identity.

Two months later, in January 1970, the naked body of a twenty-four-year-old woman was discovered by her boyfriend; again, she had been raped and strangled and had the same telltale bite marks on her breasts. The police realized that they were dealing with a serial killer, whom the media nicknamed the 'Vampire Rapist' due to the savage bite marks on all the victims. Montreal was hit by a wave of fear. This third murder, however, was his last for the time being and the killer disappeared, perhaps due to the rising awareness of the case. Nearly eighteen months later, in May 1971, Elizabeth Porteus, a teacher, failed to turn up for work at her high school in Calgary, Alberta. The school contacted her apartment owner, who checked on Porteus and found her dead on her bedroom floor. She had been raped and strangled and had bite marks on her breasts. During the savage attack not only had her apartment been left with considerable damage but, crucially, one of her killer's cufflinks had been broken and dropped, which the police discovered under her body. Enquiries led to the discovery that the teacher had been recently dating a man known as Bill and the two had been seen in a car together on the night of her murder.

Boden was arrested and convicted on the evidence of the bite marks left on all the victims after Gordon Swann, a local orthodontist, eventually identified 29 areas of similarity between a cast of Boden's teeth and the marks left on Elizabeth Porteus, the first time this form of evidence was used in a prosecution. Indeed, such was the rarity of such a method being used that Swann could find no examples on which to base his work in Canada and after applying to the FBI for help, he eventually turned to an English expert who had worked on this method in the past. Boden was sentenced to life imprisonment in February 1972 and died of skin cancer in prison in March 2007.

Was Boden any more of a vampire than Haigh or Kurten? The only link between him and vampirism is the fact that he bit his victims, but not on the throat. Why not instead link him to a ferocious animal that bites its prey, such as a wolf or a lion, for example? On reflection, it is necessary to take the 'vampire' traits from all three cases (the night attacks on women, the biting of the victim and the drinking of blood) before any real comparison can be made between the killers and vampires, and even then this is only the relatively modern image of the vampire from literature or the cinema. Let us consider the time period of the three examples, the period between 1920 and 1970. This is the prime period for vampire cinema and encompasses the films *Nosferatu*, *Dracula* (Lugosi) and *Dracula* (Lee). Is this a mere coincidence? What the heavily influential cinema imagery of the vampire allowed for was the capability to recognize vampiric traits throughout society. Therefore, the vampire being was transformed once again into a scapegoat for the horrors that mankind is capable of, and this is by no means dissipating as our knowledge and understanding of the vampire grows.

In the present many of the examples of vampirism relate to cases of sadistic 'vampire crime', and disturbingly these are becoming more and more frequent. In North Wales in November 2001 sixteen-year-old Matthew Hardman murdered a ninety-year-old woman named Mabel Leyshon. What is horrific about this case is that Hardman stabbed his victim twenty-two times, mutilated her body and placed pokers in the shape of a cross at her feet.[12] He then cut out her heart, wrapped it in newspaper and placed it inside a pan on a silver platter at the side of her body. After this, he drank her blood. In the trial the prosecution claimed that Hardman was 'obsessed with vampires and the occult' and had told friends that he wanted to kill someone 'to become immortal'.[13] Two months before the murder Hardman had accused a sixteen-year-old German girl of being a vampire, and had asked her to bite his neck so that he could become a vampire too.[14]

In 2005 Channel 4 aired a programme entitled 'The Real Vampire Chronicles' which detailed the vicious murder in Scotland in December 2002 of Thomas McKendrick by his close friend Allan Menzies. Menzies stabbed McKendrick 42 times with a bowie knife before battering his head with a hammer, drinking his blood and eating part of his head.[15] He did this, he claimed, because the queen vampire Akasha from Anne Rice's novel *Queen of the Damned* ordered him to, although three independent psychiatrists examined him and found him to be completely sane. Both Hardman and Menzies were found guilty of murder and were sentenced to a minimum of twelve years in prison.

If a person conforms to certain vampiric traits, for example, if they shun daylight, carry out vampiric acts and consume blood, then are they not technically a vampire? They may not be an undead vampire, but then ultimately, this form never really existed outside of people's imaginations and fears. It took society a long time to accept that the vampire was not real and yet, rather curiously, once they did, the vampire was brought to life. Although both these cases involved vampiric acts, in particular the drinking of blood, neither featured traditional vampire beings, although it could be argued that both killers wished to become vampires. However, it is only the modern depictions of vampires that suggest one must drink blood in order to be 'turned' into a vampire – this in itself is evidence that the age-old vampire traditions, associations and folklore are lost. In December 2004, in Birmingham, England, reports began circulating that a real-life vampire was roaming the streets and attacking members of the public,[16] which terrified locals, even after the police insisted the allegation was a myth. The reports claimed that in the Glen Park Road area of Ward End a 'vampire' bit a male pedestrian and then attacked the residents who came to his aid. These reports, however, were rather short and random and no names of the 'sources' were provided. The *Birmingham Evening Mail* ran an article that claimed 'as the sun dips below the rooftops of sleepy terraced streets, residents rush home, quickly gathering up playing children, because after night falls a vampire hungry for blood stalks. Reports of a Dracula-style attacker on the loose biting innocent people has spread terror throughout neighbourhoods in Birmingham, causing many to fear the darkness of the night'.[17] The suggestion of a 'Dracula-style' attacker is interesting – was he really the caped and fanged aristocrat from the books and films? Or were people merely latching on to preconceived ideas? A 'biting attacker' must be a vampire and a vampire must be akin to Dracula; such is popular opinion.

This suspicion is further supported by the fact that the police had no suspects in the case and there were no hospital reports of bite victims. So did a 'vampire' really prowl the streets or was it merely the result of hearsay and urban myths? Let us consider the suggestion of urban myths for a moment and Stuart Jeffries' comparison to that of 'Spring-heeled Jack' of

1830s London.[18] Eyewitness accounts apparently told of a tall man wearing a long, black cloak who breathed blue flames from his mouth. Yet further accounts told how 'Jack' had horns and cloven feet and was the offspring of the Devil. There is a pattern emerging here: the tall, cloaked 'Jack' of the 1830s reports shares similarities with a similarly attired 'Jack' of London in the 1880s, and the vampires of the period and on into the following century were also akin to this image. Jeffries further suggests that these vampires that occur in modern society are no longer the charismatic Counts of Transylvania but rather 'hip, sexy, immortal teens' and it is perhaps this image that draws people into emulating their actions in cases of vampiric crime.

Father Marcus Stock, director of schools for Birmingham's Catholic diocese, suggests that modern television programmes, such as *Buffy the Vampire Slayer*, *Charmed* and *Sabrina the Teenage Witch*, which are aimed at impressionable teenagers, are being adopted as a spiritualistic replacement of the Christian faith. As it could certainly be argued that the Church is losing its influence over the younger generation, one can understand his concern.[19] That a vampire was prowling Birmingham's streets is obviously untrue, but what is interesting is that many people believed, or wanted to believe, that it was. Although if there really was a 'vampire' stalker it was most likely some disturbed attacker, the continued ability of the vampire to 'appear' in modern society is a reflection of the importance of this most fabled of myths. In February 2005 the *Birmingham Evening Mail* ran another story claiming the police had arrested a suspect in the case, but this point tends to be omitted from the 'sensational vampire stories' that surround the incident.[20]

Across Europe there are still examples of more 'traditional' cases of vampires like the one from Birmingham, and nowhere more so than in the vampire heartland of Eastern Europe. The most famous are two examples from Serbia and Romania respectively.

In March 2007 news reports claimed that a Serbian man, Miroslav Milosevic, had been arrested after driving a hawthorn stake into the grave and through the heart of the former Yugoslavian dictator Slobodan Milosevic in the Serbian town of Prozaevac. The 'vampire hunter' (who was no relation to the former dictator) claimed that he had done this to stop him returning from the dead.[21]

This act may seem a little bizarre but it occurred deep in the heart of Eastern Europe, and vampire traditions still hold their roots firm in this part of the world. In 2001 the Governor of the Yugoslavian Central Bank, one Mladjan Dinkic, likened Slobodan Milosevic to a vampire as he was 'politically dead' but continued to 'suck the blood of Serbia'.[22] The *Sunday Herald* further suggested that the act, which was carried out just under a year to the day that Milosevic died (he died on 11 March 2006), follows Balkan traditions in that the *Vampire Hunter's Almanac*, a Balkan vampire hunter manual, states that the first anniversary of a suspected vampire's death is extremely significant.[23] The article further suggested that although Milosevic was dead, he was still 'haunting' the Yugoslavian people, and upon calling the police from the inside of the tomb to inform them of his intentions, the young vampire hunter was warned to take care as the hand of Milosevic might get him from the grave.

In December 2003 in the Transylvanian village of Marotinu de Sus, Petre Toma, head of the Toma family, died and was buried in the village cemetery.[24] Although Petre had no traditional Romanian 'vampire signs' prior to his death, his niece suffered nightmares and claimed her uncle was visiting her from the grave and feeding from her heart (note, not her blood), and became ill. The cemetery Petre was buried in is typical of rural Romanian cemeteries and allowed easy access to the graves; many were not sealed in order to allow for future family interments, leaving gaps between the tomb and the capstones. Visible skulls and bones of the dead must have created a macabre scene for any visitor, but not for the locals. Small hearths on each grave allowed for food and wine to be brought for the deceased, because Romanian belief states that the dead are afraid of the dark and get hungry and thirsty. On his visit to the village and the cemetery, the archaeologist Timothy Taylor spoke to a local man, Niculae Pedescu, who narrated the events of the Toma case.

On 8 January 2004 the corpse of Petre Toma was investigated and deemed to be a *strigoi*. At midnight the following night the body was disinterred and cut open and the heart removed. The tools used for this were, incredibly, a large scythe and a pitchfork. The heart was then transported, on said pitchfork, through the village to the crossroads where the villagers roasted it and captured the charred flakes in a towel. These were then mixed in a glass of water and Toma's niece drank the liquid. The next morning she felt much better.[25] Reaction to the case was mixed, although the peasant villagers were only carrying out what they believed were justified age-old folkloric traditions. Romania's acceptance into the European Union and the push for modernization by her European contemporaries created an air of hostility and repulsion towards the act and the people involved. For, apart from the tourism factor, Romania continues to downplay its role within the vampire genre. Toma's brother was given a custodial sentence for the sacrilegious act, although this was later commuted, thanks to the argument by the Romanian social anthropologist Mihai Fifor that it was part of wider peasant traditions.

These traditional forms of vampire belief are difficult to find in the West, where suggested examples of vampirism tend to relate to acts of violence, torture, murder and crime. The only examples of note are those in Seán Manchester's work.[26] The most famous of the vampire cases involving Manchester is that relating to the Highgate Vampire, which is discussed in more detail in the next chapter. In a conversation between myself and Seán Manchester he suggested that many cases of 'traditional' vampires do actually occur in the West but that the wide-scale interest and related events surrounding the Highgate case had taught him, and presumably other 'vampire hunters', to keep their activities out of the public eye, so as to avoid the problems he faced when hunting the Highgate Vampire.[27]

Nevertheless, there is one other case that has attracted public interest, that of the so-called Kirklees Vampire, which is reported to haunt the Kirklees Estate in West Yorkshire, England. Kirklees is, according to legend, the burial place of the infamous outlaw Robin Hood. Folklore suggests that after the death of Maid Marion, Robin was himself wounded in a skirmish with the Sheriff's men. Robin made his way to Kirklees, the suggested home of his cousin the Prioress, where he hoped to be bled by her in order to save him from his wound. For some reason unbeknown to us the Prioress bled Robin to death (some versions of the Robin Hood stories, such as Henry Gilbert's, suggest that the Prioress was in league with Robin's enemy, Sir Roger of Doncaster, and had made a pact with him to kill Robin. This cannot be conclusively accepted, given that the stories differ from version to version), and his body was buried under a great stone in the grounds of Kirklees.

From the 1980s onwards reports of strange, supernatural incidents and sightings began to circulate, which prompted Seán Manchester to investigate. The following account is from the *Brighouse Echo*: 'Like a bat she hung there for what seemed like an eternity, her black nun's robes flapping eerily while her eyes flashed red and venomous and her teeth bared sharp and white between snarling blood-red lips'.[28]

Other strange occurrences include one visitor to the site collapsing in the tower near the tomb and needing mouth-to-mouth resuscitation; a researcher for the *Yorkshire Life* becoming ill after visiting the site, leaving her paralysed from the neck down for two weeks afterwards; and a reporter for the same magazine claiming she had been pulled to the floor by some sort of force near to the grave.[29]

Manchester also stated that a number of blood-drained animals were discovered near to the grave, and upon inspection the grave appeared to have several finger-wide holes in the earth directly on top of the tomb.[30] This latter point has similarities within vampire folklore, where it is suggested that vampires can leave their graves at night through the smallest hole, and that small, finger-wide holes are often found on graves of prospective vampires. Manchester's investigation of the case involved himself and two colleagues visiting the grave of Robin Hood and the Prioress' tomb in 1990 and performing an exorcism after hearing a shrieking noise and witnessing a darkly-clad woman with red eyes.

Manchester claims in his publication on the case[31] that the 'vampire' was never completely exorcised or the case solved, but that the Church and Lady Armytage, the landowner of the Kirklees Estate, requested that he withdraw his active research on the matter and consequently prevented further interest regarding the grave. One could deduce from this that either the claims of a vampire haunting the area was causing anxiety amongst the locals or that they wished to detract from the prospect of vampires in relation to the popular folk hero and his grave. It may also be the case that Manchester and his companions were becoming a nuisance with regards their presence and 'vampire hunting' and were also creating 'bad press' for the Church, particularly as Manchester was himself a priest.

The question that must be addressed is whether the Kirklees case is actually a case of vampirism in the traditional sense. That is, is the Kirklees Vampire really a vampire at all? In *International Vampire* (Issue 10), regarding the Kirklees case, it is stated that robbers and highwaymen, people who were victims of a violent death, and those who died without a priest to perform last rites and were then buried in unhallowed ground, are all prone to becoming vampires, and it could be said – if we are to believe the legends – that Robin Hood harboured all these

Sophie Lancaster
(1986–2007).

characteristics. It is certainly a romantic notion and is extremely useful from a marketing point of view, so it is easy to understand why some are keen to promote the stories of Robin Hood being a vampire. However, the many eyewitness accounts of the apparition named the Kirklees Vampire describe a female being and, if anything, this being is most likely the Prioress. The suggestion that ghostly noises belong to a vampiric Robin Hood are speculative at best.

We have examined the role of the vampire in modern society, but two further incidents show the continued resistance of society to ideas of vampiric, Goth and 'dark' culture. This is no more evident than in the sickening account of the attack on two young Goths in Lancashire in 2007. In the early hours of 11 August, Sophie Lancaster and her boyfriend Robert Maltby were walking through the skate park area of Stubby Lee Park, Bacup, when they were attacked. The vicious assault that took place, between

1.10 am and 1.20 am, left both victims unconscious and bleeding heavily from their ears and noses, with Miss Lancaster having a piece of her scalp missing where the attackers had ripped out her hair.[32] In fact, such was the ferocity of the attack the investigating officer, Detective Inspector Dean Holden of Lancashire police, reported that the injuries were so severe that they were initially unable to tell which of the two was female and which was male.[33] Five youths were later arrested over the incident. All five later pleaded guilty to 'grievous bodily harm with intent' and two, Ryan Herbert and Brendan Harris, were found guilty of murder.

Detective Inspector Holden further commented that, although a motive of robbery could not be ruled out as some of the victims' belongings were missing, the most likely cause of the attack was that the pair were 'Goths'; both had been dressed in Goth attire on the night of the attack. Robert Maltby later came out of his coma in North Manchester general hospital and is now recovering, but, sadly, Sophie Lancaster died as a result of her injuries on 24 August 2007. That the police believed the attack could have been attributable to a 'hate crime' due to the pair's Goth appearance was further supported when it was suggested they had been previously targeted for abuse due to their dark clothing and piercings.[34] Tributes for Sophie poured in from across the world, not just from the Goth community but from all areas of society, including a number of music concerts, memorials, a commemorative bench in Whitby and a website dedicated to Sophie's memory.

There remains a close link between the varying subcultures, particularly the Gothic trend, vampires and the horror genre in general, and many people are persecuted within society because of this. It is extremely unlikely that Sophie's killers would have differentiated between any of the varying subcultures anyway, and generally people who dress in dark or black clothing, wear dark make-up and listen to Goth, metal or rock music tend to be viewed as being 'Goths'.

Although nowhere near as tragic as the case of Sophie Lancaster, in February 2007 the media released a string of stories relating to a teacher from Accrington, Lancashire who was subjected to a media furore after it was discovered she was also a part-time author who had released vampire-themed novels. A headline in *The Sun* claimed she was a 'vampire teaching our kids' and that she had a 'lurid fascination with VAMPIRES' (article's emphasis).[35] Samantha Goldstone, under the alias Paigan Stone, also had an internet site that contained 'provocative images' and 'adult content with vampire eroticism, violence and blood lust'. A spokesperson for the teaching union NASUWT commented that 'in writing lurid material as a teacher, you'd struggle to maintain professionalism amongst impressionable young people'.[36] Samantha Goldstone's work may have been deemed inappropriate by the media, but it does not make her a vampire. Yet with headlines like this, Goldstone has been instantly transformed by the press from a Gothic author into a blood-drinking fiend.

Are these last two examples any different to the persecutions witnessed in the witch trials of the Middle Ages or the angry mob of *Varney, the Vampyre*? In modern society, one would expect a little tolerance of social groups or sub-cultures, but sadly, this is not always the case. Out of the examples discussed, only one (the teacher) has any real link with vampires and her stories were certainly not harmful, especially compared with the examples of desecration or murder evident in some of the others. It is only when vampirism becomes real and seems to infiltrate our everyday lives that the fear we once had of vampires is rekindled, a factor that is readily apparent in the only case of vampirism witnessed on such a scale since the mass hysteria of the eighteenth-century vampire epidemics, that of the infamous Highgate Vampire of London.

# Vampiric Haunts #3: Highgate Cemetery, London, England

Throughout history, when such forces have been unleashed, they
have been known to cause havoc and destruction, disease and
death. Conjuring forth these devilish entities is the work of black
magic whose devotees will stop at nothing in their abuse of
Creation, bringing chaos to the natural order of things.

Seán Manchester, *The Highgate Vampire*

Reports of a strange supernatural entity that began to circulate
around London in the late 1960s and early '70s marked the
beginning of one of the strangest events in London's history: a
real-life vampire hunt that would last nigh-on thirty years. At the
head of this were two men: the priest, historian, poet and mystic
Seán Manchester and David Farrant, President of the British
Psychic and Occult Society. Both men claim to have seen the
entity, named 'The Highgate Vampire' due to its vampire-like
appearance of a dark shape with glowing red eyes (similar to the
Kirklees Vampire). Farrant was supposedly among the first to
witness the being in February 1970 and described it as 'a seven
foot tall figure just inside the top gate of the cemetery',[1] and the
nightmares of one Elizabeth Wojdla, later investigated by
Manchester, agreed: 'we heard a low vibrating noise – like a slow
booming sound . . . suddenly, a dark shape moved across the
path directly in front of us'[2] and 'I think I see the face of a wild
animal with glaring eyes and sharp teeth, but it is a man . . .'.[3]

Whether these accounts and the subsequent events caused
by them are evidence of a real vampire can perhaps never be
proven, but they were definitely the catalyst for a long-lasting
vampire hunt and continued media and public interest. The

fact that a priest so wholeheartedly puts forward the idea that he not only believed in the Highgate Vampire but also twice tracked it down and eventually destroyed it,[4] and with wide public interest, suggests that the idea of vampirism is still socially relevant. Before we look at the case in more detail, it is necessary to understand the history and nature of Highgate Cemetery itself and how this was able to lend itself to the case.

## HIGHGATE CEMETERY

The area that Highgate Cemetery covers has a long and curious history; as far back as the fourteenth century, a castle was situated in the Highgate area, with much of the surrounding land used for hunting deer. By the sixteenth century, however, the castle lay in ruins and was much overgrown, but the area was later developed with a number of gentleman's houses, one of which was purchased and renovated by Sir William Ashurst and became Ashurst House. After his death in 1720 the house was allegedly sold to a 'mysterious nobleman from the Continent who arrived in the wake of the vampire epidemic',[5] after which came reports of strange incidents, such as stories of a tall, grey figure hovering in the moonlight.

The house was eventually sold and demolished and the land was used to build the present church of St Michael, with the rest of the estate lands being bought by the London Cemetery Company. The gardens of the house were used for what is now the Western cemetery at Highgate and, in true Victorian style, became a popular and fashionable place of rest with elegant catacombs, monuments and mausoleums. A vast number of famous and influential people have been buried there, including Karl Marx, Douglas Adams, George Eliot, Sir Donald Alexander Smith and Michael Faraday.

The cemetery of Highgate was itself one of seven cemeteries opened in London (nicknamed 'The Magnificent Seven') in

Highgate Cemetery, London.

the early nineteenth century, and by the end of that century it is reported that around 100,000 people had made provision to be buried there. The culmination of the two World Wars and the consequent lack of money meant that the cemetery fell into disrepair, and the scene today is one of decay. The dense foliage and undergrowth appear to swallow the hundreds of tombstones and grave markers, many of which are damaged. At the time of the Highgate Vampire case, in the late 1960s and early '70s, the scene was much worse, with tombs lying open, revealing the grisly remains of bodies and skeletons falling out of their caskets. Reports of vandalism in the cemetery even detailed how the young were making their way into the cemetery at night and removing bodies from graves and tombs and in some instances dancing with them in macabre 'dares'. Fortunately, if nothing else, the Highgate case brought public attention to the dilapidated state of the cemetery and an effort was made to return the cemetery to some of its former glory. Restoration work by the Friends of Highgate Cemetery and a five-year project with

177

the Manpower Services Commission along with finance from English Heritage have meant that all the major buildings and several of the monuments have been restored or conserved and the area is now a listed Grade II Park. In the year 2000 an award from Europa Nostra for conservation and restoration work was granted for work in the Lebanon Circle, the heart of the cemetery, with its circular tombs and preserved Lebanon tree.

With regards to the cemetery's supernatural history, there are further suggestions from Victorian times of a tall man, but this time dressed in black, that would disappear through the cemetery wall,[6] and these reports are along the same lines as those given in the 1960s and '70s. All of this history, though, does not give us any associations with vampires, and only one piece of evidence, other than Stoker's work of fiction, notes vampiric qualities. It comes in the form of the story of Elizabeth Siddal, who was buried at Highgate after her death in 1855. Her husband, the artist Dante Gabriel Rossetti, wishing to obtain works of poetry buried with her, had her body exhumed in 1862 and was stunned to discover, as Charles Howell – a witness to the exhumation described – 'the undecayed body with luxuriant red-gold hair that practically filled the coffin'.[7] This would suggest that Elizabeth Siddal's body was in a state of 'undeath', and could possibly be where Stoker got his idea for the Highgate / Lucy Westenra episode.

Though it is difficult to explain this phenomenon, it is interesting to note that the area known as Church Yard Bottom in Highgate's Queen's Wood was used as a burial ground for plague victims in the fifteenth century, and as has been discussed earlier, there are links between vampirism and plague burials.

Highgate Cemetery also has a history of occult practices and Satanism:

Remains of a weird ceremony in the murky depths of the catacombs were also discovered. Evidence included pieces of burnt crucifixes, dried blood, splashes of black candle grease and traces of a curious mixture which when analysed turned out to be deadly nightshade, rue, myrtle covered in sulphur and alum, the majority of which had been burned.[8]

In his investigation of the case, Manchester further suggested that 'it should be remembered that the link between our world and that of the undead is found in Satanism and the black arts.'[9] Could he be suggesting therefore that it was occult practices that unleashed the entity that became the Highgate Vampire? Farrant's view on the case also suggests an occult link:

One particular tomb . . . had been converted into a small Temple and, judging from the inverted pentagram and magical symbols inscribed on the floor and walls, was in regular use . . . the particular signs and symbols used could only be applicable in a Rite dedicated to one of the most malign Deities to rule amongst the Old Kings of Hell . . . no amateur would be capable of calling forth this Deiform. In fact, in accordance with Satanic belief, this entity could only be summoned to the earthly plane if it was to perform some mission, and could not 'return' until that mission had been fulfilled.[10]

Whether this practice of dark arts bears any relevance to the Highgate Vampire is uncertain, but it is no less credible than the idea of ghosts, vampires or the undead. Farrant also put forward the idea that the awakening of the dormant vampire could have been a subconscious result of the occult rituals and that the intention was never to awaken it. The story in the *Hampstead & Highgate Express*[11] entitled 'Why do the foxes die?' appeared all too willing to push the vampire idea and this could well have been one of the sources for the myth, as a vampire in

Highgate Cemetery would have been big business in a journalistic sense. The story relates to the number of dead foxes drained of blood found in the cemetery that were initially linked to the practice of Satanism and then used as evidence of the existence of a vampire (again, much like Manchester's other notable case of the Kirklees Vampire). Now, there are problems with both of these theories: firstly, if those involved in secret acts of black magic did use the foxes in a sacrificial sense they would hardly be likely to leave them lying in the pathways to be discovered; and secondly, a vampire would also be unlikely to drink the blood of foxes when, according to eyewitness reports, he had confronted numerous people and had harmed none, let alone drunk their blood. It seems strange that the vampire would prefer animal blood to human, given all the history and folklore on the subject. It is therefore easy to believe that the dead foxes were deliberately placed there to be discovered in order to fuel the vampire stance on the matter. An interesting point is that both Farrant and Manchester, the two so-called vampire hunters, are both willing to blame the vampire for the foxes' deaths and neither consider them to be publicity stunts.

### MANCHESTER VS FARRANT

The two most prominent people in the case of the Highgate Vampire are without doubt Seán Manchester and David Farrant, two people who have written about their own attempts to hunt the Highgate Vampire. They have battled for supremacy over the last 30 years. Some would suggest that the two continually attempt to popularize their own involvement in the case whilst deriding the other's, but from reading their accounts one gets the feeling that it is Manchester who is the main instigator of the feud; 'few amateur vampire hunters were less qualified than Farrant and none caused more trouble. Farrant was so much an amateur as to be comic'.[12] The reason for this is that, in Manchester's eyes, Farrant has constantly sought the limelight by continually changing his stance on the case and misrepresenting the facts for his own purposes. Farrant, on the other hand, never mentions Manchester in his account in the *Highgate Vampire Casebook Files* of 2005 entitled 'The Highgate Vampire – How it all began', and it is in the introduction to this by Catherine Fearnley that we hear of 'the claims of certain others who attempted to "cash-in" on the official investigation by claiming that the reported figure must be a "blood-sucking vampire". We must assume here that the 'certain others' is Manchester, as he invariably claims that the Highgate entity was a vampire, whilst Farrant tends to promote the supernatural spectral explanation and claims to have only agreed to the being's vampiric qualities, in his words, 'when pushed'. Yet in Manchester's recorded interview with Farrant in 1978,[13] Farrant was asked 'You took it upon yourself to fulfill the ancient and approved method by which one might destroy the Undead being. Is this so?' to which Farrant replied 'Yes'.

By Fearnley's comment on the 'official investigation', she is suggesting, and this is supported by Farrant, that the exorcism or killing of the vampire was supposed to be carried out by Farrant. Yet Manchester claims it was he who carried it out, with Farrant being nothing more than an amateur vampire hunter. Manchester[14] clears this up somewhat in that he discusses a letter sent by Farrant to the *Ham & High* in 1970 stating how he (Farrant) had seen the apparition but that he had 'no knowledge in this field and would be interested to hear if any other readers have seen anything of this nature'.[15] It is hard to imagine someone with 'no knowledge in this field' being asked to undertake an official investigation. In *Beyond the Highgate Vampire*, Farrant's 1991 pamphlet (revised in 1997) that gives his account of the Highgate Vampire case, Farrant claimed to be a white witch who saw the so-called vampire more as another sort of supernatural being; yet in the 1978 interview Farrant agreed that in 1970 he was a freelance vampire hunter who sometimes worked with others (some of these being Satanists). When asked if he himself was a Satanist, he replied that he would not describe himself one way or the other but that he could see the difference in black and white magic, with him being more on the white side. Manchester openly admits his certainty of the entity being a vampire and at times appears a little over the top and far-fetched in his reports of events, but this could possibly be due to the fact that he is a devout Old Catholic priest and an admirer of the perhaps first 'priestly vampire-hunter' Reverend Montague Summers. In *The Vampire Hunter's Handbook* he goes as far to say that some see Summers being his precursor in the field of vampirology.[16] Indeed, it does appear that Manchester was on some great religious crusade to rid the world of the vampire's evil in his reports from the 1970s and one cannot help feeling that his actions were somewhat built-up to make for a better story.

Returning to Farrant there are further contradictions in his story, most notably the fact that in 1993 he set up the Highgate Vampire Society to 'become a repository for all the oral history and written data concerning the Highgate Vampire',[17] which appears strange, given that he had stated that he did not believe the being to be a vampire. In the introduction to Farrant's work, Fearnley again defends him, saying that he was not in the cemetery for vampire hunting, and yet in an article in the *Evening News* the journalist Barrie Simmons reported:

I joined a macabre hunt . . . for the vampire of Highgate Cemetery. David [Farrant], 24, was all set, kitted out with all the gear required by any self-respecting vampire hunter. Clutched under his arm, in a Sainsbury's carrier bag, he held the tools of his trade. There was a cross made out of two bits of wood tied together with a shoelace and a stake to plunge through the heart of the beast. Vampire hunting is a great art. There is no point waiting for the monster to appear. It must be stalked.[18]

Farrant was arrested and jailed for five years in 1974 for tomb vandalism largely on photographic evidence (including the so-called 'Nude Rites' picture) found in Farrant's house, depicting himself in certain tombs adorned with occult symbolism and a full-frontal nude picture of his then girlfriend Martine de Sacy posing in the tomb, damning evidence for his links with black magic. In his defence, Farrant explained that he and some friends had gone to the tomb to expose the Satanic symbology and whilst there found a pentagram with a bust of the deceased (whose tomb it was) in the centre. They decided to perform some sort of exorcism to combat the work of the Satanists; Farrant proceeded to read excerpts from the Bible and spells from other ancient works and the female visitors removed their clothes 'for purity'.[19] After this they left, but not before Farrant had taken some photographs of the symbology (and de Sacy) to show to the police and as a record of his 'exorcism'. This photograph of de Sacy, rather unfortunately for Farrant, later resurfaced and did him no favours in his quest to clear his name. So was Farrant merely the victim of a misunderstanding by the police? It appears too coincidental that Farrant was arrested on numerous occasions for 'illegal acts' in or around Highgate Cemetery and was ultimately prosecuted, and his continually changing stories and versions of events did him no favours. Add this to the fact that Manchester was never in trouble with the police, even though according to his accounts it was he who performed exorcisms, gained entry to graves and tombs on several occasions and ultimately 'destroyed' the vampire, and it is therefore difficult not to take Manchester's side in the proceedings.

Incidentally, Farrant's current view on the foxes is that there is no evidence to link the incident to the vampire, but that they could be seen as a 'chilling reminder' to the episode in *Dracula* where a vampiric entity (Lucy Westenra, the so-called 'bloofer lady') wandered Hampstead and was responsible for attacking children.[20] Yet another curious statement, given his refusal to call the being a vampire.

### THE HIGHGATE VAMPIRE

After the initial reports, Manchester's investigation into Elizabeth Wojdyla's nightmares and Farrant's arrest, it was the fox incidents that sparked the Highgate Vampire proceedings. The conclusion of the 'fox' article was 'the mysterious death of foxes in Highgate Cemetery was this week linked with the theory that a ghost seen in the area might be a vampire'.[21] (For the purpose of discussing the events it is Manchester's account that shall be considered given that he seems, of the two, the most reliable witness.) After the *Ham & High*'s article a number of people contacted Manchester on the subject, including two sisters named Anne and Lusia. It was Anne herself that asked for Manchester's help as Lusia was suffering from episodes of sleepwalking and on following her one night Manchester ended up at Swains Lane and proceeded into the grounds of St Michael's church. He was led to a tomb within Highgate Cemetery where he claims a grey haze obscured his view, which then cleared, to be followed by a low booming noise, whereby he quickly rescued Lusia and took her home.

The following weeks brought further reports, including five separate accounts of a tall man in a hat. One account claimed that the man had walked through a wall and another that the apparition was accompanied by the eerie sound of church bells.[22] Further accounts described a ghostly cyclist, an apparition walking into a pond and two accounts of a strange woman in white.[23] Ellis' theories on these alleged sightings link them with wider-known legends, such as the headless horseman, and traditions surrounding lakes, rivers, ponds and drowning. In February 1970 an article in the *Ham & High* asked 'Does a Wampyr walk in Highgate?'[24] This may have been a sarcastic take on the claim that the Highgate being was not just a vampire, but a King Vampire from Wallachia that had made its way to London in a coffin in the seventeenth century. *Dracula*, anyone? Joking aside, the suggestion of a vampire at large in Highgate was perhaps just the 'spooky'[25] cover needed for the more sinister allegations of devil-worshipping, black magic and occult practices that Manchester and Farrant believed had set the vampire free. Indeed, it was only really Manchester who pushed for the 'vampire' theory and other work on the subject tends to lean towards an occult explanation. The evidence of desecrated graves, dismembered bodies and Satanic symbolism found throughout the cemetery over a sustained period seems to suggest that the area was being used by people practising the Dark Arts, and one has to wonder whether the vampire theory was in fact welcomed by these people as it gave them a useful cover story.

Nevertheless, the vampire theory was adopted and public fear rose to such an extent that a reader known only as M. M. was quoted in the *Ham & High*:

> Does a vampire walk in Highgate? It is no more fantastic than the supposition of a ghost or phantom that so many readers amply attest to witnessing . . . must we exhume the ghost? Well, if Seán Manchester's theory of a vampire is correct, I would have thought the sooner it was exorcised the better. The question then remains, who would dare handle the job?[26]

On 13 March 1970, it was agreed, Manchester would exorcise the vampire. Once this became public knowledge, however, the way was laid for a whole gaggle of amateur vampire hunters to flock to Highgate Cemetery in pursuit.

On the eve of the proposed vampire hunt, Thames Television sent a crew to record an interview with Manchester and
set up at the north gate on Swains Lane. As recording com-
menced a strange noise interfered with the sound, the camera
director fainted suddenly and the wind howled through the
trees, causing the generator wires to lash violently on the ground
and the producer's notes to fly all over the place.[27] If this
account is true, it is more reminiscent of a supernatural occurrence than anything vampiric.

When Manchester went to the catacomb with two assistants
for the exorcism, he again heard the booming noise, but this
eventually stopped. He was able to gain access to the tomb,
where he found three empty coffins in which he placed garlic
and a cross. A disturbance in the cemetery, due to hundreds of
spectators congregating outside, caused the police to intervene
and the vampire hunt was abandoned, but again the following
weeks brought further reports and sightings until on 7 August
1970 a headless body and signs of a Satanic ceremony were
discovered near to the area where Lusia's sleepwalking had led
Manchester back in March.[28] He returned with Lusia and some
assistants and hypnotized her so he could question her, whereupon she entered a trance and repeated the phrases 'where are
you?' and 'I'm coming' over and over. She eventually led him to
a tomb in the Lebanon Circle, which he gained entry to and discovered the vampire in a coffin, describing it as a 'form gorged
and stinking, with the life-blood of others . . . the glazed eyes
stared horribly, almost mocking me. Under the parchment-like
skin a bluish tinge could be detected. The colour and appearance of the face suggested a corpse of no more than three days
. . . yet the vault was more than a century old'.[29] He attempted
to stake the vampire but conscience deterred him and they left
after placing garlic, holy water and a crucifix within the vault. He
then made a circle of salt and placed cups of holy water outside
the vault, performed an exorcism and sealed the vault with

The tomb of the Highgate vampire.

antidotes mixed within the mortar. (On visiting the cemetery in 2006, I noted that the vault has since been re-opened.) Manchester finishes his account by claiming that his Bible had fallen open at Deuteronomy and he noted the words 'Only be sure that thou eat not the blood: for the blood is the life'.[30]

Criticism of Manchester's accounts were rife in the aftermath of the alleged exorcism. Bernard Davies noted that Manchester's original account in 1970 and his updated version of events in *The Vampire's Bedside Companion* (1975) differed in that in the new account the vampire in the Lebanon Circle vault had 'red, glowing eyes' and 'long, pointed fangs clotted with stained blood' and that the entrance to the tomb was sealed with garlic in the mortar although this was not mentioned in the original (1970) account.[31] Davies also stated that any hard evidence had conveniently disappeared. Manchester's reply to this was that he did have evidence in the form of photographs and testimonies but that Davies chose to ignore these. He does not explain, however, the additions to the later accounts.

Dorothy Nixon, in the 1978 issue of the American *Journal of Vampirism*, further challenges Manchester in that she discusses the bite marks of Elizabeth Wojdyla. Her problem lies with the fact that the bites are arranged vertically rather than horizontally as would be expected. This is because a vampire would bite in one of three ways; by pinching the skin with both upper and lower fangs on one side of the mouth, by biting with both upper fangs (in the way that snakes bite), or by biting with both lower fangs. She suggests that the second and third methods are impossible with the human mouth, as the incisors would obstruct the bite due to the curvature of the mouth. She further believes that because of the shape of the human neck, a vertical bite would be impossible, so any bite must be horizontal. Martin Riccardo, editor of the *Journal of Vampirism*, suggested, however, that based on the ghostly structure of the vampire attested in the eyewitness accounts, it would be possible for a vertical bite as he believes vampires to be transmorphic (shape-shifters) and therefore able to angle their teeth in this way. Manchester defended his work by stating that he has demonstrated, using a live model, that incisors can indeed bite in the way that would be necessary for the marks left on

Elizabeth Wojdyla and on Lusia, who also suffered similar bite marks.

He also believes that vampires live 'outside of time' and that this allows for some of the previously unexplained phenomena attributed to vampires:

> [Whilst recognising a state of] anti-matter, that is matter made up of atoms consisting only of anti-particles, unable to exist in the presence of normal matter . . . we often fail to recognise anti-time where a counter-time unfolds opposite to all normal time. We are familiar with only three dimensions and the sequence of time trapped within them. But these concepts of normal time – past, present and future – are non-existent in anti-time. The conscious energy of the undead exists outside all ties of time. Hence no shadow, nor any reflection and sometimes the power to change shape.[32]

It is an interesting theory, but it relies on the premise that an undead being has the power and knowledge to be able to travel between expanses of time. Assuming the Satanic rituals had inadvertently unlocked this gateway, how is the undead being able to exist in both dimensions, *time* and *anti-time*? Since it has the *anti-time* possibilities of no shadow or reflection, how is it possible for it to interfere with people or objects living in a dimension of *time*?

Manchester's exorcism of the Highgate Vampire ended the reports and incidents in the cemetery itself, but somehow the vampire allegedly survived and sought solace in a house on Crescent Road on the borders of Highgate and Hornsey, nicknamed by the press the 'House of Dracula'. This time, Manchester did stake the vampire through the heart and destroyed it. He has photographs of the vampire's rapid decay once staked. No further reports of the vampire have been forthcoming.

There are certain similarities between the Highgate case and events in *Dracula*, and while these could well be down to wider vampire typologies such as found in aspects of folklore, the coincidences are readily apparent. Events such as Lusia visiting the cemetery and Elizabeth Wojdyla's nightly visitation are similar to the experiences of Lucy Westenra, as is Lusia's sleep-walking episode. Manchester's description of the exorcism in Highgate Cemetery, where he left Lusia in a circle of salt, mirrors the actions of Van Helsing towards the end of *Dracula* when he leaves Mina Harker in a circle of salt in Transylvania, and his mention of a patient escaping from Priory Hospital only to be killed (possibly by the vampire) is suggestive of Renfield, the psychiatric patient who is killed by Count Dracula.[33]

When Manchester goes to the 'House of Dracula' to hunt the vampire he is aided by a person known as Arthur; Arthur Holmewood is one of the characters who hunts Dracula. A final similarity is that Manchester claimed that after he had staked the vampire, he went to an eighteenth-century masquerade ball and was re-acquainted with Anne, the sister of Lusia. Earlier at the party, Manchester saw Lusia through the crowd, but Anne said this could not be possible as Lusia had become ill and passed away. Sightings of a vampire then occurred in the Great Northern London Cemetery and this turns out to be Lusia, who must have been infected by the Highgate Vampire before its demise. This is extremely similar to Lucy Westenra returning as the 'bloofer lady' in *Dracula* after having been bitten by the Count to haunt Highgate Cemetery in the novel, but surely it would have been too much for Lusia (remarkably close to Lucy) to have returned to Highgate for her vampiric hauntings?

In summary, then, the Highgate case may well have had nothing to do with vampires at all, but the theory conveniently rose as a cover for more sinister occult practices. The reports of devil worshipping and Satanic rituals, the desecrated graves and dismembered bodies, the general run-down state of the cemetery and the eagerness by people such as David Farrant and Seán Manchester to become involved in a bizarre 'vampire hunt' may have influenced people's alleged 'sightings' of a ghostly figure. Ideas on ghosts and vampires gleaned from television and cinema, not to mention the continuous media hype, probably created a kind of 'snowball effect' as regards the reports. After all, if everyone is talking of the supposed vampire, and newspapers and television are full of supposed sightings and theories, a visitor to the vicinity of Highgate would already have a large proportion of subconscious imagery inside their head, and it would only take a fleeting shadow or the movement of a bird or a fox in the undergrowth to provoke paranoia. For this to be created, though, society had to have a clear idea of vampires, their characteristics, haunts and associations and the case is crammed full of traditional vampire imagery; the cemetery, the coffins, the fangs, the garlic and the stake. And obviously all the sightings and incidents had to occur at night.

If Manchester is to be believed and he did finally destroy the 'vampire', there should be no further sightings of the being. Manchester himself assured me that there have been no such sightings and that any suggestion to the contrary are mere hearsay, and yet there are further reports of 'vampiric activity' at Highgate. In September 1978 the Wessex Association for the Study of Unexplained Phenomena announced they would hold a vigil at the tomb of a suspected vampire,[34] and just a couple of days later a gang of youths were arrested for 'riotous and indecent behaviour'.[35] They later admitted to having read the earlier newspaper article and decided to join the 'hunt' themselves, and were caught by the police banging on tombstones with stakes shouting, 'Come out vampire, we are coming to get you'.[36] Ellis adds to this the fact that every Halloween people flock to the cemetery to carry out vampire hunts,[37] suggesting that the vampire association with Highgate remained well into the 1990s, and possibly even to this day.

# Conclusion: A Dark Reflection of Human Society?

We have seen that the vampire has taken on many forms throughout history before finally adopting that which we know so well in the present. The modern vampire sleeps in his coffin throughout the daylight hours, waking come sunset to stalk his prey and drink its blood. And yet was his path from ancient demon to modern-day fanged fiend inevitable, given all the examples discussed? Was his evolutionary transformation a constant progression through history and culture?

One must here determine whether there is a definite link between each form; for example, was it inevitable that the spirit form of the vampire's early history would one day metamorphose into a more 'solid' being (in this case, the revenant)? If it is decided that no single common attribute of vampires, such as blood-drinking, shape-shifting or rising from the grave, is necessary, then it is reasonable to suggest that either a) there is another conclusive 'ever-present' factor or b) there is in fact no link and therefore no evolutionary pattern. It is the author's opinion that there can be seen to be no defining link in *all* examples of vampirism except for the aspect of fear, and it is this point that the fundamental elements of any doctrine must be based upon.

The neurologist and psychoanalyst Ernest Jones in his *On the Nightmare* goes some way to explaining the relationship between death and fear:

a continued relation between the living and dead may be regarded in two ways, and each of these from the obverse and reverse. On the one hand it may be desired, and this may result in either the living being drawn to the dead or in the dead being drawn back to the living; on the other hand it may be feared, which may also have the two same effects.[1]

The progression that we witness in arriving at the modern myth, then, is the spirit or demon form evident in the ancient world followed by a cross-over in the prehistoric period where shifting funerary beliefs depict clear associations between the physical dead and the spiritual dead. This leads in turn to the idea of the revenant, or undead being, that could be trapped on earth after death (caused by many factors, often area-specific) with a progressive route apparent from this point up to the modern creation: through the Medieval period, the epidemics of the eighteenth century, the Gothic literature of the nineteenth century and finally the 'fixed', modern form we are familiar with.

Many people regard literary examples as the basis of the modern vampire myth, and although this is a fair assumption in many respects, these themselves were influenced and based upon much earlier foundations, as we have seen. The early reports of the eighteenth-century epidemics were seen as the first documentary evidence of vampires, and yet medieval writers such as Walter Map or William of Newburgh (see Appendix) provided documentary examples some 500–600 years previously. In essence, it all depends on how exactly one defines the term 'vampire'.

Many works on vampires tend to concentrate their analysis on the latter phase of vampirism, the period from the early eighteenth century to the end of the nineteenth, culminating in *Dracula* and responses and critiques of this.[2] They do, however, acknowledge the earlier history of vampirism but do not usually dwell on this for too long. Although the word 'vampire' did not enter the English language until 1736 (and so in effect prior to this point there were no 'vampires' per se), it is impossible to deny that early demons and revenants are precursors of the 'vampire'. Thus it is equally important to consider these in detail in any vampire history.

Aside from the popular imagery and the elements that are associated through the varying cultures or periods we must also consider what the vampire *represents*. If the modern vampire image is the culmination of a historical evolution based on fear (and fascination with death), then once this fear began to subside what we are left with is fascination with the being and with death, and this is evident in many cases of vampire crime. It is this factor that Ernest Jones pointed out above; that the relationship between the living and the dead, or life and death, can be maintained so long as *desire* or *fear*, or both, are present. If one replaces the other, such is apparent in the modern examples, would it then be expected that the representation of a vampire may also change? This goes back to the suggestion earlier that the vampire is for some the 'ultimate villain' (or Stuart Jeffries' 'hip, sexy, immortal teen'). However, there is something remarkably more fundamental in society's interest with vampires, and this is our desire for ever-lasting life. The lure of the vampire is often that he cannot die (so long as he feeds on the life-force of blood, energy, etc) and society's attempt to emulate this is often apparent. We have noted the many examples of using blood as a rejuvenator throughout history, and in the present this act is still evident in the extreme cases of vampiric torture or murder, where the killer consumes the victim's blood in order to obtain their life. It would be difficult to surmise that interest in the vampire's immortality could only begin to form after society overcame its fear of the being, as in order to seek to emulate the vampire a person must first hold the belief that not only is the vampire powerful and dominant but that in being these things he must instill fear in others. It is, perhaps, a kind of catch-22: the vampire needs the fear in order to remain dominant but while the fear remains we cannot expect to empathize with him and thus become like him.

The quest for immortality is by no means a phenomenon exclusive to vampirism and examples are far-reaching within society. Examples include the miraculous healings of Jesus and, ultimately, his resurrection from death, the quest for the Holy Grail, *The Portrait of Dorian Gray*, tales of revitalising springs, and examples from mythology such as Achilles or the Gorgons from Greek Mythology and the mythical Phoenix who would rise from the flames of its own death to live again. Interestingly, there are often ways in which an immortal being can die. In the *Highlander* films this could be done by cutting off an immortal's head, and with vampires there are numerous ways such as the stake through the heart, or sunlight, and this tends to suggest that although we are deeply interested in the dream of immortality it is tantalizingly beyond our grasp.

The second *Cambridge Dictionary* entry for *immortal* is 'someone who is so famous that they are remembered for a long time after they are dead' and in this the vampire is all-conquering, even though he was never alive in the first place. Richard Dawkins continues on this thought when he commented that you do not actually die as long as some of your genetic material is left behind,[3] and although this is true for us mortal humans, it is not so necessary for the immortal vampire. It is an illusion that a would-be vampire needs to consume the blood of others to obtain immortality. Granted, the process of drinking or using blood has been linked with life throughout history, but generally this idea is due to a belief in its healing or rejuvenating powers rather than its ability to prolong life. Consuming the blood of the enemy after battle would, it is believed in certain cultures, give the consumer his victim's power and strength and the emerging medical practice of blood transfusion that matured alongside the later vampire literature enforced the idea of the life-power of blood. It is more likely that this was the reason why consuming blood became a paradigm of vampirism as opposed to any great quest for immortality. For instance, take the traditional folkloric view of the vampire being in Eastern Europe; here, we witness an attempt to extract a victim's 'energy', rather than blood, to empower the vampire. But, the power of literature and cinema eventually mutated this 'power draining' into something more horrific, and thus the blood-drinking fiend was immortalized.

If we consider the principle of a baby suckling its mother to obtain milk in order to grow, then this is remarkably similar to the manner in which a vampire feeds in order to maintain life. The difference here lies in the fact that babies suckle the breast whereas, traditionally, it is the neck that the vampire feeds from. But this is not exclusively the case throughout examples of vampirism. In *Dracula* Stoker's Count forces Mina to drink his blood from a wound on his chest and in *Nosferatu* Count Orlock attempts to drink Hutter's blood from the cut he suffers to his finger. The fact that in both these films we also see the more traditional method of obtaining the blood from the neck must suggest that it is the consumption of blood that is important, regardless of which part of the body it is obtained from. Studies of the feeding habits of babies suggests that the baby associates the breast with feeding but as they are then moved to the shoulder area for winding, they associate the neck with frustration, as although they must temporarily refrain from feeding in order to be burped, they are in fact still hungry and can sometimes continue the suckling motion against the flesh of the neck.[4] Miller further suggests that what we have here is a target area through association for the suppressed anger a child feels when an inadequate level of feeding has taken place or perhaps when a child is simply hungry. Is this, then, the subconscious foundation for the vampiric act?

Let us now, finally, consider the only other known being that feeds exclusively on blood, the *Desmodus rotundus* or common vampire bat, first given its vampire tag by European explorers who discovered them in South America.[5] There are in fact three types of vampire bat, the other two are *Diaemus youngi* (white-winged vampire bat) and the *Diphylla ecaudata* (hairy-legged vampire bat). The main difference, with regards prey, is that the latter two types tend to opt for wild birds and fowls whereas the common vampire bat hunts larger mammals such as horse, pig or cow. In order to obtain this blood the vampire bat either lands on the back of its host or carefully approaches it on the ground, using its feet and thumbs to creep up. Once on the host, the bat feeds by using a heat-sensing organ on its face to detect where the blood vessels are closest to the surface. The vampire bat then cuts the skin using its small, sharp front teeth and laps at the blood with its tongue. To prevent the blood clotting, an anti-coagulant is released into the wound.

The vampire bat's bodily system is so precise that if it does not feed every two or three days it can die from starvation. Once a bat has fed, it often returns home to regurgitate part of the meal in order to feed other members of the roost. This could well be the source for the myth that vampires must continually feed to maintain their vampiric strength and power. Much like the mythical creature that shares its name, the vampire bat is often misunderstood and persecuted. In some instances explosives have been put in bat caves by fearful locals in the mistaken belief that the bats were actually vampires.[6] Today, because of the destruction of vampire bats most often due to their mis-association with the vampiric being, they are quite rare and only inhabit areas in Trinidad, Central America and the northern part of South America.

To try to understand the habits of the vampire bat, the BBC made a film in 1979 entitled 'Vampire', which documented the bats in Trinidad. Trinidad was chosen because of the number of

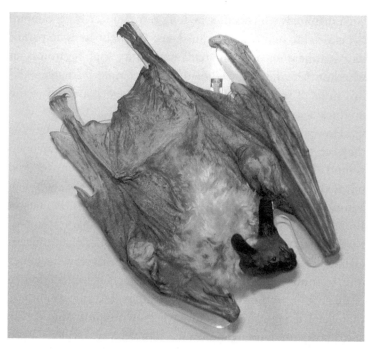

*Desmodus rotundus,* the vampire bat.

attacks by vampire bats on humans in the 1950s and '60s, a particular concern due to the threat of rabies. The BBC crew located a local farmer who owned a donkey that was being attacked
by vampire bats on an almost nightly basis and set up a base in
the donkey's stall. For the first few nights no bats came; the
crew attributed this to their lights scaring the bats off. They
soon realized that it was in fact the moon that was keeping the
bats at bay. On bright, moonlit nights the vampire bats
remained in the shadows and had to hunt their prey in the forest, but once the sky turned overcast, the bats appeared and
attacked the donkey. Because of the anti-coagulant, the blood
continued to flow, but due to the size of the victim the blood-
loss caused no real damage. A smaller animal may have suffered
more and one wonders whether this is why the bats attack only

large mammals which suffer no long-term impact. The vampire bat is also the only known animal who willingly gives up part of its own meal in order to feed one of its kin, regardless of whether the other bat is a relative or a complete stranger, and this in itself is a far cry from the cruel image portrayed of the mythical vampire.

However, a vampire bat attack is not without its dangers as they can often transmit rabies through their saliva into an open wound. This is not only bad news for the animals they feed on but also for the humans they attack from time to time. Although a human attack is rare, they do happen occasionally. In 2005 in Brazil twenty-three people died from rabies as a result of vampire bat attacks in a two-month period.[7] Brazilian officials claimed that around 1,300 people had been treated for rabies due to 'unusually serious' vampire bat attacks attributed to deforestation in the Amazon. Another possible suggestion was that the bat population could have grown rapidly due to the spread of cattle farming in the area, and mass attacks have been known in Latin America in the past when cattle have been suddenly removed. The bats' food source was denied to them so a replacement had to be found.

Although the vampire is a mythical being, vampire bats prove that it would technically be possible for a creature to not only feed on human blood, but to live exclusively from this. Couple this with the mass hysteria and vampire epidemics that were finding their way into the West at roughly the same time as explorers were returning with tales of blood-sucking creatures that came out at night and attacked people spreading deadly diseases, and the foundations for the widespread phenomenon was set. As no-one had actually *seen* a vampire in the West, the being was able to metaphorically 'shape-shift' into whatever guise society's imagination could conjure.

There is no typical vampire. Perhaps a 'true' vampire would be an amalgamation of all the forms we have seen worldwide as well as reflecting attributes of all the historical examples. In essence, the vampire reflects an ever-changing being that bears relevance to the culture it exists in. The modern vampire is a being born of demons, burned as a heretic and reviled as a fiend; the Devil's own creation. What the future may hold for him is uncertain, yet it is undeniable that the image immortalized by *Dracula*, encapsulating over six thousand years of history, can never be undone.

How blessed are some people,
Whose lives have no fears, no dreads,
To whom sleep is a blessing that comes nightly,
And brings nothing but sweet dreams.

Bram Stoker, *Dracula* (1897)

APPENDIX:

# Historia Rerum Anglicarum
# ('History of English Affairs')

*Historia Rerum Anglicarum* was written by William of Newburgh and covers the period between 1066 and 1198. The version used is from *The Church Historians of England*, volume IV, part II, trans. Joseph Stevenson (1861).

## BOOK 5

CHAPTER 22: Of the prodigy of the dead man, who wandered about after burial

[1] In these days a wonderful event befell in the county of Buckingham, which I, in the first instance, partially heard from certain friends, and was afterwards more fully informed of by Stephen, the venerable archdeacon of that province. A certain man died, and, according to custom, by the honorable exertion of his wife and kindred, was laid in the tomb on the eve of the Lord's Ascension. On the following night, however, having entered the bed where his wife was reposing, he not only terrified her on awaking, but nearly crushed her by the insupportable weight of his body. The next night, also, he afflicted the astonished woman in the same manner, who, frightened at the danger, as the struggle of the third night drew near, took care to remain awake herself, and surround herself with watchful companions. Still he came; but being repulsed by the shouts of the watchers, and seeing that he was prevented from doing mischief, he departed. Thus driven off from his wife, he harassed in a similar manner his own brothers, who were dwelling in the same street; but they, following the cautious example of the woman, passed

the nights in wakefulness with their companions, ready to meet and repel the expected danger. He appeared, notwithstanding, as if with the hope of surprising them should they be overcome with drowsiness; but being repelled by the carefulness and valor of the watchers, he rioted among the animals, both indoors and outdoors, as their wildness and unwonted movements testified.

[2] Having thus become a like serious nuisance to his friends and neighbors, he imposed upon all the same necessity for nocturnal watchfulness; and in that very street a general watch was kept in every house, each being fearful of his approach unawares. After having for some time rioted in this manner during the night-time alone, he began to wander abroad in daylight, formidable indeed to all, but visible only to a few; for oftentimes, on his encountering a number of persons, he would appear to one or two only though at the same time his presence was not concealed from the rest. At length the inhabitants, alarmed beyond measure, thought it advisable to seek counsel of the church; and they detailed the whole affair, with tearful lamentation, to the above-mentioned archdeacon, at a meeting of the clergy over which he was solemnly presiding. Whereupon he immediately intimated in writing the whole circumstances of the case to the venerable bishop of Lincoln, who was then resident in London, whose opinion and judgment on so unwonted a matter he was very properly of opinion should be waited for: but the bishop, being amazed at his account, held a searching investigation with his companions; and there were some who said that such things had often befallen in England, and cited frequent examples to show that tranquillity could not be restored to the people until the body of this most wretched man were dug up and burnt. This proceeding, however, appeared indecent and improper in the last degree to the reverend bishop, who shortly after addressed a letter of absolution, written with his own hand, to the archdeacon, in order that it might be demonstrated by inspection in what state the body of that man really was; and he commanded his tomb to be opened, and the letter having been laid upon his breast, to be again closed: so the sepulcher having been opened, the corpse was found as it had been placed there, and the charter of absolution having been deposited upon its breast, and the tomb once more closed, he was thenceforth never more seen to wander, nor permitted to inflict annoyance or terror upon any one.

## CHAPTER 23 – Of a similar occurrence at Berwick

In the northern parts of England, also, we know that another event, not unlike this and equally wonderful, happened about the same time. At the mouth of the river Tweed, and in the jurisdiction of the king of Scotland, there stands a noble city which is called Berwick. In this town a certain man, very wealthy, but as it afterwards appeared a great rogue, having been buried, after his death sallied forth (by the contrivance, as it is believed, of Satan) out of his grave by night, and was borne hither and thither, pursued by a pack of dogs with loud barkings; thus striking great terror into the neighbors, and returning to his tomb before daylight. After this had continued for several days, and no one dared to be found out of doors after dusk – for each dreaded an encounter with this deadly monster – the higher and middle classes of the people held a necessary investigation into what was requisite to he done; the more simple among them fearing, in the event of negligence, to be soundly beaten by this prodigy of the grave; but the wiser shrewdly concluding that were a remedy further delayed, the atmosphere, infected and corrupted by the constant whirlings through it of the pestiferous corpse, would engender disease and death to a great extent; the necessity of providing against which was shown by frequent examples in similar cases. They, therefore, procured ten young men renowned for boldness, who were to dig up the horrible carcass, and, having cut it limb from limb, reduce it into food and fuel for the flames. When this was done, the commotion ceased. Moreover, it is stated that the monster, while it was being borne about (as it is said) by Satan, had told certain persons whom it had by chance encountered, that as long as it remained unburned the people should have no peace. Being burnt, tranquillity appeared to be restored to them; but a pestilence, which arose in consequence, carried off the greater portion of them: for never did it so furiously rage elsewhere, though it was at that time general throughout all the borders of England, as shall be more fully explained in its proper place.

## CHAPTER 24 – Of certain prodigies

[1] It would not be easy to believe that the corpses of the dead should sally (I know not by what agency) from their graves, and

should wander about to the terror or destruction of the living, and again return to the tomb, which of its own accord spontaneously opened to receive them, did not frequent examples, occurring in our own times, suffice to establish this fact, to the truth of which there is abundant testimony. It would be strange if such things should have happened formerly, since we can find no evidence of them in the works of ancient authors, whose vast labor it was to commit to writing every occurrence worthy of memory; for if they never neglected to register even events of moderate interest, how could they have suppressed a fact at once so amazing and horrible, supposing it to have happened in their day? Moreover, were I to write down all the instances of this kind which I have ascertained to have befallen in our times, the undertaking would be beyond measure laborious and troublesome; so I will fain add two more only (and these of recent occurrence) to those I have already narrated, and insert them in our history, as occasion offers, as a warning to posterity.

[2] A few years ago the chaplain of a certain illustrious lady, casting off mortality, was consigned to the tomb in that noble monastery which is called Melrose. This man, having little respect for the sacred order to which he belonged, was excessively secular in his pursuits, and — what especially blackens his reputation as a minister of the holy sacrament — so addicted to the vanity of the chase as to be designated by many by the infamous title of "Hunde-prest," or the dog-priest; and this occupation, during his lifetime, was either laughed at by men, or considered in a worldly view; but after his death — as the event showed — the guiltiness of it was brought to light: for, issuing from the grave at night-time, he was prevented by the meritorious resistance of its holy inmates from injuring or terrifying any one with in the monastery itself; whereupon he wandered beyond the walls, and hovered chiefly, with loud groans and horrible murmurs, round the bedchamber of his former mistress. She, after this had frequently occurred, becoming exceedingly terrified, revealed her fears of danger to one of the friars who visited her about the business of the monastery; demanding with tears that prayers more earnest than usual should be poured out to the Lord in her behalf as for one in agony. With whose anxiety the friar — for she appeared deserving of the best endeavors, on the part of the holy convent of that place, by her

frequent donations to it — piously and justly sympathized, and promised a speedy remedy through the mercy of the Most High Provider for all.

[3] Thereupon, returning to the monastery, he obtained the companionship of another friar, of equally determined spirit, and two powerful young men, with whom he intended with constant vigilance to keep guard over the cemetery where that miserable priest lay buried. These four, therefore, furnished with arms and animated with courage, passed the night in that place, safe in the assistance which each afforded to the other. Midnight had now passed by, and no monster appeared; upon which it came to pass that three of the party, leaving him only who had sought their company on the spot, departed into the nearest house, for the purpose, as they averred, of warming themselves, for the night was cold. As soon as this man was left alone in this place, the devil, imagining that he had found the right moment for breaking his courage, incontinently roused up his own chosen vessel, who appeared to have reposed longer than usual. Having beheld this from afar, he grew stiff with terror by reason of his being alone; but soon recovering his courage, and no place of refuge being at hand, he valiantly withstood the onset of the fiend, who came rushing upon him with a terrible noise, and he struck the axe which he wielded in his hand deep into his body. On receiving this wound, the monster groaned aloud, and turning his back, fled with a rapidity not at all interior to that with which he had advanced, while the admirable man urged his flying foe from behind, and compelled him to seek his own tomb again; which opening of its own accord, and receiving its guest from the advance of the pursuer, immediately appeared to close again with the same facility. In the meantime, they who, impatient of the coldness of the night, had retreated to the fire ran up, though somewhat too late, and, having heard what had happened, rendered needful assistance in digging up and removing from the midst of the tomb the accursed corpse at the earliest dawn. When they had divested it of the clay cast forth with it, they found the huge wound it had received, and a great quantity of gore which had flowed from it in the sepulchre; and so having carried it away beyond the walls of the monastery and burnt it, they scattered the ashes to the winds. These things I have explained in a simple narration, as I myself heard them recounted by religious men.

[4] Another event, also, not unlike this, but more pernicious in its effects, happened at the castle which is called Anantis, as I have heard from an aged monk who lived in honor and authority in those parts, and who related this event as having occurred in his own presence. A certain man of evil conduct flying, through fear of his enemies or the law, out of the province of York, to the lord of the before-named castle, took up his abode there, and having cast upon a service befitting his humor, labored hard to increase rather than correct his own evil propensities. He married a wife, to his own ruin indeed, as it afterwards appeared; for, hearing certain rumors respecting her, he was vexed with the spirit of Jealousy. Anxious to ascertain the truth of these reports, he pretended to be going on a journey from which he would not return for some days; but coming back in the evening, he was privily introduced into his bedroom by a maid-servant, who was in the secret, and lay hidden on a beam overhanging, his wife's chamber, that he might prove with his own eyes if anything were done to the dishonor of his marriage-bed. Thereupon beholding his wife in the act of fornication with a young man of the neighborhood, and in his indignation forgetful of his purpose, he fell, and was dashed heavily to the ground, near where they were lying.

[5] The adulterer himself leaped up and escaped; but the wife, cunningly dissembling the fact, busied herself in gently raising her fallen husband from the earth. As soon as he had partially recovered, he upbraided her with her adultery, and threatened punishment; but she answering, "Explain yourself, my lord," said she; "you are speaking unbecomingly which must be imputed not to you, but to the sickness with which you are troubled." Being much shaken by the fall, and his whole body stupefied, he was attacked with a disease, insomuch that the man whom I have mentioned as having related these facts to me visiting him in the pious discharge of his duties, admonished him to make confession of his sins, and receive the Christian Eucharist in proper form: but as he was occupied in thinking about what had happened to him, and what his wife had said, put off the wholesome advice until the morrow — that morrow which in this world he was fated never to behold! — for the next night, destitute of Christian grace, and a prey to his well-earned misfortunes, he shared the deep slumber of death. A Christian burial, indeed, he received, though unworthy of it; but it

did not much benefit him: for issuing, by the handiwork of Satan, from his grave at night-time, and pursued by a pack of dogs with horrible barkings, he wandered through the courts and around the houses while all men made fast their doors, and did not dare to go abroad on any errand whatever from the beginning of the night until the sunrise, for fear of meeting and being beaten black and blue by this vagrant monster. But those precautions were of no avail; for the atmosphere, poisoned by the vagaries of this foul carcass, filled every house with disease and death by its pestiferous breath.

[6] Already did the town, which but a short time ago was populous, appear almost deserted; while those of its inhabitants who had escaped destruction migrated to other parts of the country, lest they too should die. The man from whose mouth I heard these things, sorrowing over this desolation of his parish, applied himself to summon a meeting of wise and religious men on that sacred day which is called Palm Sunday, in order that they might impart healthful counsel in so great a dilemma, and refresh the spirits of the miserable remnant of the people with consolation, however imperfect. Having delivered a discourse to the inhabitants, after the solemn ceremonies of the holy day had been properly performed, he invited his clerical guests, together with the other persons of honor who were present, to his table. While they were thus banqueting, two young men (brothers), who had lost their father by this plague, mutually encouraging one another, said, 'This monster has already destroyed our father, and will speedily destroy us also, unless we take steps to prevent it. Let us, therefore, do some bold action which will at once ensure our own safety and revenge our father's death. There is no one to hinder us; for in the priest's house a feast is in progress, and the whole town is as silent as if deserted. Let us dig up this baneful pest, and burn it with fire.'

[7] Thereupon snatching up a spade of but indifferent sharpness of edge, and hastening to the cemetery, they began to dig; and whilst they were thinking that they would have to dig to a greater depth, they suddenly, before much of the earth had been removed, laid bare the corpse, swollen to an enormous corpulence, with its countenance beyond measure turgid and suffused with blood; while the napkin in which it had been wrapped appeared nearly torn to pieces. The young men, however, spurred on by wrath, feared not,

and inflicted a wound upon the senseless carcass, out of which incontinently flowed such a stream of blood, that it might have been taken for a leech filled with the blood of many persons. Then, dragging it beyond the village, they speedily constructed a funeral pile; and upon one of them saying that the pestilential body would not burn unless its heart were torn out, the other laid open its side by repeated blows of the blunted spade, and, thrusting in his hand, dragged out the accursed heart. This being torn piecemeal, and the body now consigned to the flames, it was announced to the guests what was going on, who, running thither, enabled themselves to testify henceforth to the circumstances. When that infernal hell-hound had thus been destroyed, the pestilence which was rife among the people ceased, as if the air, which had been corrupted by the contagious motions of the dreadful corpse, were already purified by the fire which had consumed it.

# REFERENCES

## Introduction

1 *BBC News*, 23 December 2002, http://news.bbc.co.uk/1/hi/ world/africa/2602461.stm.
2 Christopher Frayling, *Vampyres: Lord Byron to Count Dracula* (London, 1991).
3 Quoted in Jan Perkowski, *Vampires of the Slavs* (Columbus, OH, 1976).
4 Frayling, *Vampyres*, p. 34.
5 Wayne Bartlett and Flavia Idriceanu, *Legends of Blood* (Stroud, 2005), p. viii.
6 Delia Grigore, 'Vision Patterns for the Representation of the Sacred and Habitual Means of Relationship with the Supernatural in the Rroma Traditional Culture', a paper given at the Symposium of the Transylvanian Society of Dracula, 2006.
7 Dom Augustin Calmet, *Treatise on the Vampires of Hungary and Surrounding Regions* (Southend, 1993).
8 As put forward by Frayling, *Vampyres*.
9 Bishop D'Avranches Huet, quoted in Wright, *The Book of Vampires* (London, 1924), p. 9.
10 Archbishop Giuseppe Davanzati, quoted in Frayling, *Vampyres*, p. 30.
11 For Rousseau's take on the vampire phenomenon, see *Lettre à Christophe de Beaumont* (Pleiade, t.iv, 1969) and his initial first draft of *Emile* (*Profession de Foi*), ed. Masson (Paris, 1914).
12 Wright, *Book of Vampires*.
13 Jean-Baptiste de Boyer, *Lettres Juives* [1738] (Provence, 1990).

ONE

# The Ancient World: Origins of the Vampire

1 Philostratus, *Life of Apollonius of Tyana*, trans. F. C. Conybeare, book IV, p. xxv.
2 Montague Summers, *The Vampire: His Kith and Kin* (London, 1928).
3 Wayne Bartlett and Flavia Idriceanu, *Legends of Blood* (Stroud, 2005).
4 Leviticus 17:10–14.
5 Dudley Wright, *The Book of Vampires* (London, 1924), p. 19.
6 This was famously depicted in the hit movie *Indiana Jones and the Temple of Doom* (1984). The suppression and integration of India into the British Empire led to the demise of the Thuggee cult in the 1800s and was one of the factors in contributing towards Indian acceptance of British rule.
7 Innana Arthen, *An Exploration of the Greek Vrykolakas and His Origin* (unpublished, 1998), p. 1.
8 An undead being, from the French *revenir,* 'to come again'. Matthew Bunson, 'Revenant', *The Vampire Encyclopedia,* (New York, 1993) p. 222.
9 See Arthen, *Greek Vrykolakas.*
10 John Lawson, *Modern Greek Folklore and Ancient Greek Religion* (New York, 1964).
11 See Lawson, *Modern Greek Folklore* and Arthen, *Greek Vrykolakas.*
12 This is also the concluding argument put forward by Arthen, *Greek Vrykolakas.*
13 Arthen, *Greek Vrykolakas.*
14 Agnes Murgoci, 'The Vampire in Roumania', *Folklore* 37 (1927), p. 320.
15 Lawson, *Modern Greek Folklore.*
16 C. F. Abbott, *Macedonian Folklore* [1903] (Chicago, IL, 1969), pp. 221–2.
17 Summers, *The Vampire.*
18 Book 7, LIII, p. 52, at http://etext.virginia.edu/toc/modeng/public/KjvLevi.html.

TWO

## The Vampire in Prehistory: Early Ideas on Death and Burial

1 *Delegation en Perse*, a French journal of antiquities. Montague Summers in *The Vampire: His Kith and Kin* (London, 1928) adds that '[the bowl is] amongst the illustrations of prehistoric utensils', p. 226.
2 Timothy Darvill, *Prehistoric Britain* (London, 1987).
3 See Miles Russell, *Monuments of the British Neolithic* (Stroud, 2000).
4 See Timothy Taylor, *The Buried Soul* (London, 2002).
5 Russell, *Monuments*.
6 Francis Pryor, *Britain BC* (London, 2004).
7 This argument is discussed in much detail in Taylor, *Buried Soul*.
8 Ross, A. and D. Robins, *The Life and Death of a Druid Prince: The Story of an Archaeological Sensation* (London, 1989).
9 Lesley Ellen Jones, 'Hi, My Name's Fox?: An Alternative Explication of 'Lindow Man's' Fox Fur Armband and Its Relevance to the Question of Human Sacrifice among the Celts', paper given at the University of California Celtic Conference, 2000.
10 See Taylor, *Buried Soul*.
11 Leslie Grinsell, *Folklore of Prehistoric Sites in Britain* (Newton Abbott, 1976), p. 20.
12 Grinsell, *Folklore of Prehistoric Sites*, p. 21.


THREE

## Historical Roots: The Vampire in the Middle Ages

1 Letter extract from Mrs Hayes to Montague Summers, June 1918, taken from Montague Summers, *The Vampire in Europe* (London, 1929), p. xi.
2 Montague Summers, *The Vampire: His Kith and Kin* (London, 1928).
3 Dante Alighieri, *Inferno* (Slough, 2006), Canto XXXIV, line 61.
4 Dudley Wright, *The Book of Vampires* (London, 1924), p. 20.

5 *Beowulf*, trans. Seamus Heaney (London, 1999), lines 104–112.
6 *Beowulf*, line 27.
7 *Beowulf*, lines 1262–9.
8 Saxo Grammaticus, *Gesta Danorum*, lines 45–6, at http://omacl.org.
9 Seán Manchester, *The Highgate Vampire* (London, 1991).
10 Constantine Gregory, *The Vampire Watcher's Handbook* (London, 2001).
11 See Appendix.
12 Matthew Bunson, '*Malleus Maleficarum*', *The Vampire Encyclopedia* (New York, 1993), p. 167.
13 Summers, *The Vampire*.
14 Cassiel Sophia, *In the Age of Ignorance* (unpublished).

FOUR

## Vampiric Haunts #1: Transylvania, Romania

1 Emily Gerard, 'Transylvanian Superstitions', in *XIX Century*, XVIII (1885), p. 130.
2 Gerard, 'Transylvanian Superstitions'.
3 Gerard, 'Transylvanian Superstitions'.
4 Agnes Murgoci, 'The Vampire in Roumania', *Folklore* 37 (1927), p. 321.
5 Such as in the case of the Highgate Vampire as reported by Seán Manchester, *The Highgate Vampire* (London, 1991) and at Danes Dyke, the Iron Age earthwork near Flamborough, North Yorkshire. Interestingly, both examples relate to the attempt by a television crew to film interviews at the locations and were reported to be small specks of dust or light swirling around in the air (in the case of Danes Dyke these were dismissed as being leaves blown by the wind, see *Bridlington Free Press* archive).
6 Murgoci, 'Vampire in Roumania'.
7 Romania today is seen as a collectivized country integrating various regions that were once separate areas in their own right, chiefly Transylvania, Wallachia and Moldova.
8 See Petr Bogatyrev, *Vampires in the Carpathians* (Columbia, SC, 1998), pp. 127–45.
9 Ibid.

10  Gerard, 'Transylvanian Superstitions'.
11  Murgoci, 'Vampire in Roumania', describes *strigoi* as the most common term for a vampire in Romania, sometimes dead, sometimes alive. *Moroi* is also used in some areas.
12  See Murgoci, 'Vampire in Roumania'.
13  Ibid., p. 136.
14  Harry Senn, 'Romanian Werewolves: Seasons, Ritual, Cycles', *Folklore* 93:2 (1982), p. 206.
15  Gerard, 'Transylvanian Superstitions', pp. 130–50.
16  Senn, 'Romanian Werewolves', p. 206.
17  The term 'mystery religion' derives from the Greek *mysterion*, to initiate, and reflects the necessity of being initiated into the cult or religion.
18  Senn, 'Romanian Werewolves', p. 206.
19  See Senn, 'Romanian Werewolves'.
20  Ibid.
21  Murgoci, 'Vampire in Roumania'.
22  Ibid.
23  Detailed in Bogatyrev, *Vampires in the Carpathians*.
24  Ibid., p. 135.
25  Murgoci, 'Vampire in Roumania'.
26  Ibid.
27  Tudor Pamfile, in *Ion Creanga* XII, 1914, p. 165.
28  Ibid.
29  Ibid.
30  Ibid.
31  Ibid.
32  The list of ways for a person to become a vampire is long. Many of the ways mentioned at this point are evident in work by Murgoci, 'Vampire in Roumania', who further suggests that many Romanians believe if a person is destined to become a vampire then they will, no matter what else may befall them.
33  Ibid.
34  Ibid.
35  Ibid.
36  Ibid.
37  Originally proposed to be built near the medieval town of Sigishoara, the birth place of Vlad Dracula in 1436, the proposal met instant opposition from environmentalists,

UNESCO, and, rather surprisingly, Prince Charles: 'large scale development would be wholly out of character within the area, and will ultimately destroy its character' (*Guardian*, 29 June 2002). Why Prince Charles should feel so passionate about the proposal is at first uncertain, but research into the British Monarchy's family tree shows that Prince Charles is actually a direct descendant of Vlad Dracula through Queen Mary (see Arlene Russo, *Vampire Nation* (London, 2005), pp. 71–2).

38 On driving through a gypsy village in northern Wallachia, my guide pointed out quantities of rocks piled outside the gates of every house. He informed me, rather incredulously, of his bewilderment at the ingenuity of the gypsy peasants: 'they are selling them! They fetch rocks from the rivers using carts and they are selling them!'

39 Raymond T. McNally and Radu Florescu, *In Search of Dracula*, (New York, 1994), p. 7.

40 E. B. Mawr, *Romanian Fairy Tales and Legends* (London, 1881), p. 111.

41 M. J. Trow, *Vlad the Impaler: In Search of the Real Dracula* (Stroud, 2003).

FIVE

## The Historical Dracula: Vlad III Țepeș

1 For more detailed biographies, see Nicolae Stoicescu, *Vlad Tepes: Prince of Wallachia*, (Bucharest, 1978), and M. J. Trow, *Vlad the Impaler: In Search of the Real Dracula* (Stroud, 2003).

2 Stoicescu, *Vlad Tepes*, p. 27.

3 *The Feast of the Impaled* is a woodcut of *c.* 1500 by Matthias Hupnuff of Strasbourg, depicting the actions of Dracula on the people of Brasov (Kronstadt). In the background can be seen the church of St Jacob (St Bartholomew in present day Brasov) which Dracula burnt in 1459 and the hill where he impaled hundreds of townsfolk in retribution for their disloyalty. Others he had executed and limbs severed or heads hacked off 'like cabbage', deeds which can clearly be seen in the foreground.

4 Trow, *Vlad the Impaler*, p. 148.

5 P. Njegos, *The Mountain Wreath*, trans. Vasa D. Mihailovich

(Vienna, 1847).

6 Herodotus, *The History of Herodotus,* trans. G. Rawlinson, Book IV, pp. 340–41. (www.classics.mit.edu//herodotus/history).

7 Trow, *Vlad the Impaler,* p. 208–9.

8 Raymond T. McNally and Radu Florescu, *In Search of Dracula* (New York, 1994), p. 88–9.

9 Translation of the Romanian story by Radu Florescu and adapted from folk tales. Ibid., pp. 208–19.

10 Ibid.

11 Trow, *Vlad the Impaler.*

12 McNally and Florescu, *In Search of Dracula.*

13 Ibid., p. 214.

14 Ispirescu, quoted in ibid., pp. 215–16.

15 Translated by Raymond McNally from MS 11/1088 in Kirillov-Belozersky Monastery Collection, in ibid., pp. 198–207.

16 Ibid.

17 As Dervla Murphy describes Romanian peasants in *Transylvania and Beyond* (London, 1993); this is by no means a derogatory term, but reflects their attitude and approach to life.

18 See McNally and Florescu, *In Search of Dracula,* p. 88.

19 Ion Bogdan, *Vlad Tepes* (1896), p. 11. The argument here is based upon the idea that Dracula had Turkish support when capturing the Wallachian throne for the second time in 1456. If this was indeed the case, why would the Treaty with Ladislaus, supposedly to safeguard against the Turks, be necessary?

20 This is from the Wallachian version by Modrussa, quoted in Trow, *Vlad the Impaler,* p. 211.

21 Tursun Bey, *Tarih-I-Ebu-I Feth-I Sultan Mehmed an,* quoted in ibid., pp. 211–12.

22 McNally and Florescu, *In Search of Dracula,* pp. 81–3, the story of Dracula and the monk.

23 Such as Stoicescu, Bogdan, etc.

24 Trow, *Vlad the Impaler* and McNally and Florescu, *In Search of Dracula.*

25 Trow, *Vlad the Impaler,* p. 145.

26 McNally and Florescu, *In Search of Dracula,* p. 85.

27 Elizabeth Miller, *Studio 2,* TV Ontario, 1996.

28 Personal communication to the author, 13 April 2007.

29 Kindly provided by Elizabeth Miller from her own private translation of Beheim's *Von ainem wutrich der heiss Trakle waida von der Walachei*.

30 *Dracula: Myth or Reality*, Official Bran Castle Tour Guide (Apostol, 2005), p. 29.

31 Miller's book *Dracula: Sense and Nonsense* (Southend, 2006).

32 The story was set in Northern Transylavania near Bistritz but Vlad Dracula was from Wallachia, although he did frequent Transylvania often. This perhaps did not bother Stoker too much; after all, he was writing a work of fiction. Alternatively, he may have been confusing the geography a little as he never actually visited the area. This does seem highly unlikely, though, given his meticulous descriptions of the area, leading to praise on the subject from people who applaud his detailed description of a region he never visited.

33 Constantin Rezachevici, 'The Tomb of Vlad Tepes: The Most Probable Hypothesis', *Journal of Dracula Studies*, IV (2002).

34 Ibid., p. 3.

35 Ibid.

36 Ibid.

37 Ibid.

38 Stoicescu, *Vlad Tepes*, p. 177.

39 Gabriel Ronay, *The Truth about Dracula* (New York, 1972), p. 93.

SIX

## From Myth to Reality: The Vampire of Folklore

1 Listed in Wayne Bartlett and Flavia Idriceanu, *Legends of Blood* (Stroud, 2005).

2 Ibid., p. 11.

3 See ibid., p. 27.

4 Personal correspondance between the author and Nicolae Paduraru, January 2007.

5 See Paul Barber, *Vampires, Burial and Death* (New Haven, CT, 1988). In certain areas of Romania funerary rites call for the body to be exhumed after seven years, when it is believed the soul has finally left the body.

6 Barber, *Vampires, Burial and Death*.

7 *BBC History Magazine*, March 2007, p. 36.

8 Barber, *Vampires, Burial and Death*, p. 42.

9 Montague Summers, *The Vampire: His Kith and Kin* (London, 1928), p. 20.

10 David Dolphin of the University of British Columbia put forward this theory in 1985 in his lecture 'Werewolves and Vampires'.

11 Tudor Pamfile, 'The Girl and the Vampire', *Ion Creanga* (1914), p. 165.

12 W.R.S. Ralston, 'The Coffin Lid', in *Russian Folk-Tales*, ed. D. L. Ashliman (London, 1873), pp. 309–11.

13 De Tournefort was a French botanist and traveller who wrote of his experiences in the Levant for the French King.

14 *Vrykolakas*, Greek vampire. Interestingly, de Tournefort puts forward his belief on the etymology and suggested meaning of the term: 'a specter carrying of a dead bod, and a Demon. Some think that vroucolakas signifies a carcase deny'd Christian burial. [From] Vrouca that nasty stinking slime which subsides at the bottom of old ditches.'

15 Joseph Pitton de Tournefort, *Relations d'un Voyage du Levant* (Lyons, 1717), vol. I, p. 142.

16 De Tournefort tells us that the townsfolk concluded that the deceased must have been a very ill man, as he was not thoroughly dead, or that he had been re-animated by Old Nick (the Devil); this is how they believed a *vroucolacas* was created.

17 De Tournefort, *Relations d'un Voyage du Levant*, p. 146.

18 Ibid., p. 147.

19 Quoted in Matthew Bunson, 'Arnold Paole', *The Vampire Encyclopedia* (New York, 1993), p. 196.

20 Translated from German by the author from Glaser's letter reproduced in Klaus Hamberger, *Mortuus non mordet: kommentierte documentation zum vampirismus 1689–1971*, p. 54–5.

21 From the report on Plogojowitz by Imperial Provisor Frombold.

22 Voltaire, *Dictionnaire Philosophique*, quoted in Christopher Frayling, *Vampyres: Lord Byron to Count Dracula*, (London, 1991), p. 31. It was during this period that radicalism became an increasing problem, particularly in France with the Jacobean revolts and in Britain where events such as the Peterloo Massacre and the Luddite machine-breaking were

all part of an extremely turbulent period. Debates on science, technological advancement and indeed vampirism suddenly outgrew their relevance within society.

## A Fiend is Born: The Vampire in Literature

1  See Paul Féval, *Le Ville-vampire*, trans. Brian Stableford [1875] (Mountain Ash, 1999), Eliza Lynn Linton, 'The Fate of Madame Cabanel', in *Appleton's Journal: A Magazine of General Literature*, VIII, 196 (1880), pp. A0005–9, Alexis Tolstoy, 'Family of the Vourdalak', [1884], in Chrisopher Frayling, *Vampyres: Lord Byron to Count Dracula* (London, 1991).

2  David J. Skal, *Vampires: Encounters with the Undead* (New York, 2006), p. 37.

3  Christopher Frayling, *Vampyres: Lord Byron to Count Dracula* (London, 1991) p. 106.

4  Frayling, *Vampyres*, p. 108.

5  The version used for this purpose is John Polidori, *The Vampyre*, 1999).

6  Many believe that the inspiration for Lord Ruthven was Byron himself. According to Skal, *Vampires*, the character was originally called Lord Strongmore, but the publisher changed this to Ruthven, based on Lady Caroline Lamb's character in her *Glenarvon* (1814). Lord Byron and Lady Lamb had previously had a disastrous love affair, but whether the switch was indeed down to the publisher or rather an intended slight on Polidori's part is still debated.

7  Polidori, *The Vampyre*, p. 1.

8  Ibid., p. 1.

9  Ibid., p. 2.

10  Ibid., p. 2.

11  Ibid., p. 10–11.

12  Ibid., p. 12.

13  Ibid., p. 15–16.

14  Ibid., p. 17.

15  Ibid., p. 20–21.

16  Ibid., p. 22.

17  Ibid., p. 25.

18  Ibid., p. 25.
19  Wayne Bartlett and Flavia Idriceanu, *Legends of Blood* (Stroud, 2005).
20  Frayling, *Vampyres*, p.108
21  Bartlett and Idriceanu, *Legends of Blood*, p. 31.
22  Montague Summers, *The Vampire: His Kith and Kin* (London, 1928).
23  *Le Vampire* by Charles Nodier.
24  Quoted in Skal, *Vampires*, p. 42.
25  *Varney, the Vampire or the Feast of Blood* was originally thought to have been penned by Thomas Preskett Prest; this error is evident in the bibliographies of many early works on vampires, including Summers' *The Vampire: His Kith and Kin*. In 1963 Louis James proved beyond doubt that the story was in fact by James Malcolm Rymer, the evidence being Rymer's own scrapbooks (see Frayling, *Vampyres*, Skal, *Vampires*).
26  The version used for this analysis is the electronic text version, courtesy of the University of Virginia Library, attributed to Thomas Preskett Prest, http://etext.lib.virginia.edu/toc/modeng/public/PreVarn.html.
27  Rymer, *Varney, the Vampyre*, Chapter 1.
28  Ibid., chapter 1.
29  Ibid., chapter 1.
30  Ibid., chapter 1.
31  Ibid., chapter 224.
32  Ibid., chapter 224.
33  Ibid., chapter 224.
34  Ibid., chapter 224.
35  Ibid., chapter 225.
36  Ibid., chapter 226.
37  Ibid., chapter 237.
38  Frayling, *Vampyres*, p. 37.
39  Skal, *Vampires*, p. 103.
40  J. Sheridan Le Fanu, *Carmilla*, taken from Daniel J. Skal, *Vampires*, (New York, 2006), pp. 103–57.
41  Ibid., chapter 4, p. 117.
42  Ibid., chapter 4, p. 118.
43  Ibid., chapter 4, p. 120.
44  Ibid., chapter 4, p. 121.
45  Ibid., chapter 6, p. 127.

EIGHT

## Vampiric Haunts #2: Whitby, North Yorkshire, England

1 Constantine Gregory, *The Vampire Watcher's Handbook* (London, 2003).
2 Bram Stoker, *Dracula* [1897] (London, 1994), p. 129.
3 Nigel Suckling, *Book of the Vampire* (unpublished, 1997).
4 Suckling, *Book of the Vampire*.
5 Juliette Wood, 'Vampires in English Fiction: Popular Tradition and Historical Sources' (2000), www.juliettewood.com/papers/vampires.pdf, p. 7.
6 Suckling, *Book of the Vampire*, p. 5.
7 Montague Summers, *The Vampire: His Kith and Kin* (London, 1928), p. 119.
8 Quoted in Christopher Frayling, *Vampyres; Lord Byron to Count Dracula* (London, 1991), p. 297.
9 This theme is discussed at great length in Frayling, *Vampyres*.
10 Ibid., p. 81.
11 Ibid.
12 Stoker, *Dracula*, p. 44.
13 Emily [de Lazowska] Gerard, 'Transylvanian Superstitions', in *XIX Century*, vol. XVIII (1885), p. 134.


NINE

## Phantasmagoria: The Modern Vampire

1 See Phillip Sugden, *The Complete History of Jack the Ripper* (London, 2002).
2 Sugden, *Jack the Ripper*, p. 2.
3 Jorg Waltje, 'Filming Dracula: Vampires, Genre and Cinematography', *Journal of Dracula Studies*, II (2000).
4 *Dracula* (1958), *The Brides of Dracula* (1960), *Dracula: Prince of Darkness* (1966), *Dracula Has Risen from the Grave* (1968), *Taste the Blood of Dracula* (1969), *Scars of Dracula* (1970), *Dracula AD 1972* (1972), *The Satanic Rites of Dracula* (1973), *The Legend of the 7 Golden Vampires* (1974).
5 *The Times*, 28 May 1958, p. 10.

6  C. A. Lejeune, *The Observer,* 1958.
7  Although this was discussed in Dion Fortune's 1930 book *Psychic Self-defence,* and has roots stemming back into the ancient cultures of Asia, China and Japan, it was Anton LaVey's (New York, 1969) work that introduced the phrase to widespread audiences.
8  Dr van Neümig, *Psychic Vampires – And How To Deal With Them,* (Imbolc, 2001).
9  For those interested in this sub-culture of vampire life-stylers, Arlene Russo's *Vampire Nation* (London, 2005) may be of interest.
10  Katherine Ramsland, 'John George Haigh', www.crimelibrary.com/serial_killers/weird/haigh/index_1.html.
11  *Daily Mirror,* 3 March 1949.
12  BBC *News* website, www.bbc.co.uk/news, 2 August 2002.
13  Ibid.
14  Ibid.
15  *Edinburgh Evening News,* 20 October 2003.
16  'Reality Bites', *Guardian,* 18 January 2005.
17  Quoted in ibid.
18  Ibid.
19  Ibid.
20  *Birmingham Evening Mail,* 8 February 2005.
21  Pakistani newspaper *The Daily Times,* 7 March 2007.
22  BBC *News* website, www.bbc.co.uk/news, 25 June 2001.
23  *Sunday Herald,* 12 March 2007.
24  Excerpt taken from the article 'The Real Vampire Slayers', *The Independent,* 28 October 2007.
25  Ibid.
26  See chapter on Highgate for a brief description of Manchester.
27  Personal correspondence between the author and Seán Manchester, September 2006.
28  *Brighouse Echo,* 12 November 1995.
29  Seán Manchester, *The Vampire Hunter's Handbook* (London, 1997).
30  Ibid.
31  Ibid.
32  *Guardian,* 25 August 2007.
33  *Lancashire Telegraph,* 12 August 2007.

34  *Guardian*, 25 August 2007.
35  *Sun*, 12 February 2007.
36  Ibid.

# TEN

# Vampiric Haunts #3: Highgate Cemetery, London, England

 1  David Farrant, 'The Highgate Vampire Society Casebook
    Files' (2005), www.davidfarrant.org, p. 1.
 2  Account of Thomas O'Loughlin in Seán Manchester, *The
    Highgate Vampire* (London, 1991), p. 54.
 3  Nightmare of Elizabeth Wojdyla after witnessing the Vampire
    in the cemetery from Swains Lane. From Manchester, *Highgate
    Vampire*, p. 55.
 4  See ibid.
 5  Ibid., p. 51.
 6  Farrant, *Highgate Vampire Society Casebook*.
 7  Ibid., p. 4.
 8  Manchester, *Highgate Vampire*, p. 65.
 9  Manchester, *Highgate Vampire*, p. 40.
10  Farrant, *Highgate Vampire Society Casebook*, p. 5.
11  6 March 1970.
12  Manchester, *Highgate Vampire*, p. 107.
13  Courtesy of Seán Manchester from the Vampire Research
    Society's archive material.
14  Seán Manchester, *The Vampire Hunter's Handbook* (London,
    1997), p. 56.
15  *Hampstead & Highgate Express*, 6 February 1970.
16  Manchester, *Vampire Hunter's Handbook*.
17  Farrant, *Highgate Vampire Society Casebook*, p. 1.
18  *Evening News*, 16 October 1970.
19  Bill Ellis, 'The Highgate Cemetery Vampire Hunt: The
    Anglo-American Connection in Satanic Cult Lore', *Folklore*,
    vol. 104, No. 1/2 (1993), pp. 13–39.
20  Farrant, *Highgate Vampire Society Casebook*.
21  *Hampstead & Highgate Express*, 6 March 1970.
22  Ellis, 'The Highgate Cemetery Vampire Hunt'.
23  Ibid.

24  *Hampstead & Highgate Express*, 27 February 1970.
25  Ellis, 'The Highgate Cemetery Vampire Hunt'.
26  Manchester, *Highgate Vampire*, p. 74.
27  Ibid.
28  Ibid.
29  Ibid., p. 86.
30  Ibid., p. 90.
31  Comments made to George Hamilton on the live 'Dracula special' show, aired from Budapest, Hungary, 27 October 1989. Davies, 1989, and quoted in Manchester, *Highgate Vampire*, pp. 96–7.
32  Manchester, *Highgate Vampire*, p. 101.
33  See Manchester, *Highgate Vampire*.
34  *Daily Express*, 9 September 1978.
35  *Daily Express*, 12 September 1978.
36  Ibid.
37  Ellis, 'The Highgate Cemetery Vampire Hunt'.

## Conclusion: A Dark Reflection of Human Society?

1  Ernest Jones, *On the Nightmare* (London, 1931), p. 398.
2  Such as Paul Barber, *Vampires, Burial and Death* (New Haven, CT, 1988), Christopher Frayling, *Vampyres: Lord Byron to Count Dracula* (London, 1991), David J. Skal, *Vampires: Encounters with the Undead* (New York, 2006).
3  Richard Dawkins, *The Selfish Gene* (Oxford, 1976).
4  Sally Miller, *Vampires, the Body and Eating Disorders* (London, 1999).
5  Adrian Warren, *The Making of 'Vampire': A film for BBC's Wildlife on One* (1979), available online at www.lastrefuge.co.uk.
6  Phil Richardson, *Bats* (London, 2004).
7  'Rabid Vampire Bats Kill in Brazil', *BBC News*, 2 November 2005.

# SELECT BIBLIOGRAPHY

Abbott, C. F., *Macedonian Folklore* [1903] (Chicago, IL, 1969)

Alighieri, Dante, *Divine Comedy* (Slough, 2006)

Apostol, D., *Dracula: Myth or Reality: Official Bran Castle Guide* (Bran, 2005)

Arthen, Innana, 'An Exploration of the Greek Vrykolakas and His Origin' (unpublished, 1998) available at http://users.netlplus.com/vyrdolak/vrykolak.htm

Barber, Paul, *Vampires, Burial and Death* (New Haven, CT, 1988)

Bartlett, Wayne and Flavia Idriceanu, *Legends of Blood* (Stroud, 2005)

Bogatyrev, Petr, *Vampires in the Carpathians* (Columbia, SC, 1998)

Bogdan, Ion, *Vlad Tepes* (1896)

Brier, Bob, *The Encyclopedia of Mummies* (New York, 1998)

Bunson, Matthew, *The Vampire Encyclopedia* (New York, 1993)

Calmet Dom Augustin, *Treatise on the Vampires of Hungary and the Surrounding Regions or The Phantom World* [1850] (Southend, 1993)

Darvill, Timothy, *Prehistoric Britain* (London, 1987)

Davies, Bernard, *Whitby Dracula Trail* (Scarborough, n.d.)

Dawkins, Richard, *The Selfish Gene* (Oxford, 1976)

De Boyer, Jean-Baptiste, *Lettres Juives* [1738] (Provence, 1990)

De Tournefort, Joseph Pitton, *Relations d'un Voyage du Levant* (Lyons, 1717)

Dolphin, David, 'Werewolves and Vampires', paper given at the annual meeting of the American Association for the Advancement of Science (1985)

Ellis, Bill, 'The Highgate Cemetery Vampire Hunt: The Anglo-American Connection in Satanic Cult Lore', *Folklore* CIV (1993)

Faulkner, R. O., *The Ancient Egyptian Book of the Dead* (London, 2006)

Féval, Paul, *La Ville-Vampire* (Mountain Ash, 1999)

Frayling, Christopher, *Vampyres: Lord Byron to Count Dracula* (London, 1991)

Gerard, Emily, 'Transylvanian Superstitions', in *XIX Century* XVIII (1885), pp.130–50

Gregory, Constantine, *The Vampire Watcher's Handbook* (London, 2003)

Grigore, Delia, 'Vision Patterns for the Representation of the Sacred and Habitual Means of Relationship with the Supernatural in the Rroma Traditional Culture', symposium of the Transylvanian Society of Dracula (2006)

Grinsell, Leslie, *Folklore of Prehistoric Sites in Britain* (Newton Abbott, 1976)

Heaney, Seamus, *Beowulf* (London, 1999)

Hirzel, S., *Deutsches Worterbuch von Jacob Grimm und Hilhelm Grimm*, 1854–1960

Jones, Ernest, *On the Nightmare* (London, 1931)

Jones, Leslie Ellen, 'Hi, My Name's Fox?: An Alternative Explication of 'Lindow Man's Fox Fur Armband and Its Relevance to the Question of Human Sacrifice among the Celts', University of California Celtic Conference (2000)

Lawson, John, *Modern Greek Folklore and Ancient Greek Religion* (New York, 1964)

Le Fanu, J. Sheridan, *Carmilla* [1872], taken from David J. Skal, *Vampires* (New York, 2006)

Linton, Eliza Lynn, 'The Fate of Madame Cabanel', *Appleton's Journal: A Magazine of General Literature*, VIII, 196 (1872), pp. A005

Manchester, Seán, *The Highgate Vampire* (London, 1991)

—, *The Vampire Hunter's Handbook* (London, 1997)

Mawr, E. B., *Romanian Fairy Tales and Legends* (London, 1881)

McNally, Raymond T., and Radu Florescu, *In Search of Dracula* (New York, 1994)

Miller, Elizabeth, *Dracula: Sense and Nonsense* (Southend, 2006)

Miller, Sally, *Vampires, the Body and Eating Disorders* (London, 1999)

Murgoci, Agnes, 'The Vampire in Roumania', *Folklore* XXVII (1927), pp. 320–49

Murphy, Dervla, *Transylvania and Beyond* (London, 1993)

Neümig, Dr van, *Psychic Vampires – And How To Deal With Them* (Imbolc, 2001)

Njegos, P., *The Mountain Wreath* (London, 1847)

Pamfile, Tudor, ed., *Ion Creanga*, XII (1914), p. 165

Perkowski, Jan, *Vampires of the Slavs* (Columbus, OH, 1976)

Polidori, John, *The Vampyre* (London, 1999)

Pryor, Francis, *Britain BC* (London, 2003)

Ralston, W.R.S., *Russian Folk-Tales* (London, 1873)

Rezachevici, Constantin, 'The Tomb of Vlad Tepes: The Most Probable Hypothesis', *Journal of Dracula Studies*, IV (2002), available at www.blooferland.com

Richardson, Phil, *Bats* (London, 2004)

Ronay, Gabriel, *The Truth about Dracula* (New York, 1972)

Ross, A., and D. Robins, *The Life and Death of a Druid Prince: The Story of an Archaeological Sensation* (London, 1989)

Russell, Miles, *Monuments of the British Neolithic* (Stroud, 2000)

Russo, Arlene, *Vampire Nation* (London, 2005)

Senn, Harry, 'Romanian Werewolves: Seasons, Ritual, Cycles', in *Folklore* ICIII (1982), pp. 206–15

Skal, David J., *Vampires: Encounters with the Undead* (New York, 2006)

Sophia, Cassiel, *In the Age of Ignorance* (unpublished, n.d.)

Stamp, C., *Dracula Discovered* (Whitby, 2001)

Stoker, Bram, *Dracula* [1897] (London, 1994)

Stoicescu, Nicolae, *Vlad Tepes: Prince of Wallachia* (Bucharest, 1978)

Suckling, Nigel, *The Book of the Vampire* (unpublished, 1997)

—, *Vampires* (London, 2006)

Sugden, Phillip, *The Complete History of Jack the Ripper* (London, 2002)

Summers, Montague, *The Malleus Maleficarum* (London, 1928)

—, *The Vampire: His Kith and Kin* (London, 1928)

—, *The Vampire in Europe* (London, 1929)

Taylor, Timothy, *The Buried Soul* (London, 2002)

Tolstoy, Alexis, 'Family of the Vourdalak' [1884], in Frayling, *Vampyres* (1884)

Trow, M. J., 'Vlad the Impaler' (London, 2003)

Voltaire, *Dictionnaire Philosophique* (Paris, 1764)

Waltje, Jorg, 'Filming Dracula: Vampires, Genre and Cinematography', *Journal of Dracula Studies* II (2000)

Warren, Adrian, *The Making of 'Vampire': A film for BBC's Wildlife on One* (1979), available online at www.lastrefuge.co.uk

Wright, Dudley, *The Book of Vampires* (London, 1924)

# WEBSITES AND MEDIA

## Online Resources (correct at February 2008)

Farrant, David, *The Highgate Vampire Society Casebook File* (2005)
www.davidfarrant.org

*Gesta Danorum* – Saxo Grammaticus
Online Medieval and Classic Library - http://omacl.org/

*Historia Naturalis* – Pliny the Elder
Online Medieval and Classic Library - http://omacl.org/

*Historia Rerum Anglicarum* – Translated by Joseph Stevenson
www.fordham.edu/halsall/basis/williamofnewburgh-intro.html

*The History of Herodotus* – Translated by G. Rawlinson
www.classics.mit.edu//herodotus/history

Leviticus – Holy Bible, King James version
http://etext.virginia.edu/toc/modeng/public/KjvLevi.html

*Life of Apollonius of Tyana* – Translated by F. C. Conybeare
www.livius.org/ap-ark/apollonius/life/va_00.htm

Ramsland, Katherine. *John George Haigh*
www.crimelibrary.com/serial_killers/weird/haigh/index_1.html

Rymer, James Malcolm. *Varney, the Vampyre, or the Feast of Blood*
http://etext.lib.virginia.edu/toc/modeng/public/PreVarn.html

Wood, Juliette. 'Vampires in English Fiction: Popular Tradition &
  Historical Sources.'
www.juliettewood.com/papers/vampires.pdf

# ACKNOWLEDGEMENTS

In writing this book I am indebted to many people, not least Dr Sarah Speight and Dr Ann Hardwick from the University of Nottingham, who offered advice and guidance in the very early stages of its conception. At various points throughout my research I had the good fortune to be aided by academics and professionals in the area of vampirology, and I must thank them all for sharing their knowledge with me. In particular I would like to thank Elizabeth Miller, President of the Canadian sector of the Transylvanian Society of Dracula, for her advice on the historical Dracula, especially where relating to the translation of Michael Beheim's work; Nicolae Paduraru, President of the Transylvanian Society of Dracula, for his views on Eastern European vampire beliefs; Dr Duncan Light of Liverpool Hope University, for his advice on the peoples of Transylvania; Bishop Seán Manchester, for kindly discussing his experience of his role as a vampirologist and providing access to the archives of the Highgate case; Cat Arnold Adams; Dr John Blair, for his preliminary paper on Anglo-Saxon vampires; Mick Smith of the London Vampyre Group and the many other people who aided in the writing of this book. Sincere thanks must go to Michael Leaman and the team at Reaktion Books for their support and belief in my work, in particular Harry Gilonis and Martha Jay, who offered guidance and advice that was instrumental in shaping this book. I would also like to thank my family, friends and colleagues who endured the best part of two years listening to me endlessly talking of vampires and other weird creatures.

Finally, I would like to thank my father for the journey into Dracula land, and my wife, Katy, who suffered endless hours of me locked away in our study and who accompanied me on many research trips. If I have missed anyone, I sincerely apologise, and stress that without the help of many people the finished work would have been unduly lacking, and that any errors are entirely my own.

# PHOTO ACKNOWLEDGEMENTS

The author and publishers wish to express their thanks to the below sources of illustrative material and/or permission to reproduce it:

Photos author: pp. 46, 54, 68, 70, 73, 74, 75, 91, 97, 108, 130, 131, 187, 199; author's collection: p. 148; photo Sir Charles Bell/© Pitt Rivers Museum, University of Oxford (PRM 1998.286.163): p. 36; Bibliothèque Nationale de France, Paris (Cabinet des Médailles, Cab. Méd. 422): p. 18; British Museum, London: p. 37; photo Paul Grover/Rex Features: p. 177; photo PA Photos, reproduced courtesy Sylvia and John Lancaster: p. 172; from Alan Saville, 'Hazleton North: the Excavation of a Neolithic Long Cairn of the Cotswold-Severn Group' (London, 1990): p. 34; photo © Warner Brothers/Everett/Rex Features: p. 6.

# INDEX